UNIVERSITY OF PENNSYLVANIA
THE MUSEUM
ANTHROPOLOGICAL PUBLICATIONS
VOL. III   NO. 1

EXCAVATIONS ON THE ISLAND OF PSEIRA, CRETE

BY

RICHARD B. SEAGER

PHILADELPHIA
PUBLISHED BY THE UNIVERSITY MUSEUM
1910

The Excavations of Richard B. Seager at Pseira and Pacheia Ammos

Philip P. Betancourt

Richard B. Seager was one of the archaeologists who worked on the island of Crete in the early years of the twentieth century. He helped to uncover the civilization we call the Minoans. The Minoan people lived on Crete during the Bronze Age, from before 3000 B.C. until they gradually merged with enough outside influences to lose their cultural identity around the year 1000 B.C. Seager excavated several sites with support from American sponsors, and he made many contributions to our knowledge of the Minoans.

Pseira

Pseira is a small islet off the coast of northeast Crete. It was excavated by Seager in 1906 and 1907. He worked both in the town and in the cemetery, uncovering parts of over fifty buildings and 33 tombs. His publication, which followed three years later, presented a summary of the discoveries.

A new excavation began in 1985 under the direction of Philip Betancourt and Costis Davaras. The new excavation contributes substantial amounts of additional evidence, and when joined to the information discovered by Seager, the projects provide a good view of the history of this rich and important harbor town.

Pseira was first settled in the Final Neolithic period. The settlers laid out the boundaries of their town on a peninsula facing toward Crete, and they built small cist graves on a hillside about 100 m west of the town as a burial-ground for their dead. The town was laid out around a Plateia, an open space surrounded by buildings on all sides. This town square, not discovered by Seager, is located in his grid squares I-J, 7-8. Irregular blocks of houses followed the natural contours of the irregular peninsula. Unlike some of the other Minoan town squares, the Pseiran Plateia was irregular, and it was not paved. A surface of bedrock, intentionally kept irregular and uneven, was used as the town's architectural focal point.

By the middle of the second millennium B.C., the town consisted of over 60 buildings. Imports from Cyprus, the Cycladic Islands, and the Near East demonstrate the foreign connections of this small seaport. Fine frescoes, elegant pottery, and objects of stone and metal testify to the wealth of the community.

Pseira was violently destroyed at the end of LM IB. A few buildings were burned, and large-scale looting took place. The town lay in ruins for a time, until smaller numbers of people re-settled it in Late Minoan IIIA. It was then abandoned again, and except for small groups of visitors, it lay in ruins until the Early Christian period when a monastery was constructed on the island.

Pacheia Ammos

The excavation at Pacheia Ammos was a "rescue excavation" undertaken to preserve ancient remains that were discovered as a result of a severe rainstorm which washed out part of the beach in the small town of Pacheia Ammos. Seager had built his home in the small village, and he was living there at the beginning of World War I. In October of 1914, a storm caused a flood that was held back by a stone wall, and when the wall was breached the resulting torrent eroded a deep gully as it made its way to the sea. The erosion uncovered a Bronze Age cemetery. Seager worked for two seasons in the excavation of the cemetery (1914 and 1915).

The cemetery at Pacheia Ammos was located on the beach, a location now covered by sand, by a road, and by restaurants. The dead were buried in jars called pithoi that were inverted and placed in holes in the ground. Most of the burials were from Late Minoan I. Offerings in the burials were scarce, but a few cups and some personal possessions were discovered.

A Note on Seager's Nomenclature

When Richard Seager worked in Crete, the nomenclature for the ceramic periods of the Minoan period was still being devised. As a result, the nomenclature used in his publications does not quite match the accepted terminology used in the late twentieth century.

1. Final Neolithic to Early Minoan I

The thick, coarse, heavily burnished pottery which was made in eastern Crete from the end of the Neolithic until the beginning of Early Minoan was not yet given a specific name in Seager's period.

2. Early Minoan

Seager helped to pioneer the pottery studies of the Early Bronze Age in Crete, and his nomenclature for EM I, EM II, and EM III is still used. When he uses these terms, they mean the same as in more modern publications.

3. Middle Minoan

The chronology of the Middle Bronze Age was not yet worked out in Seager's lifetime. He was able to distinguish early phases which he called MM I and later phases which he called MM II. Today, his MM I would be subdivided into MM IA, MM IB, and MM IIA. His later phase is MM IIB.

4. Late Minoan I

For Seager, a historical phase using both light-on-dark and dark-on-light pottery, stratigraphically below the phase of the destruction of the town of Pseira, was called MM III. Today, the end of this phase would be called LM IA. Its beginning would be in MM III, but the difference between the two phases is still not clearly differentiated in this part of Crete. The phase Seager called LM I is called LM IB today.

5. LM II and LM III

The later pottery of the Late Bronze Age was not yet distinguished at the time Seager was excavating these sites.

6. Roman and Byzantine

In 1907 when Seager excavated at Pseira, the difference between Late Roman and Early Byzantine pottery was not yet recognized. Everything at Pseira which Seager called Roman is actually Byzantine.

CONTENTS

EXCAVATIONS ON THE ISLAND OF PSEIRA, CRETE

THE DISCOVERY OF THE SITE AND THE SEASON'S WORK.

Our attention was first called to the Minoan settlement on the island of Pseira in 1903, when we learned from a Turkish boatman of the existence there of old walls and potsherds. On visiting the spot it was clear that we had to do with a town similar to that at Gournia, but as Mrs. Hawes was then occupied with the excavations at that site, no trial was made until 1906, when, after a short season at Vasiliki, I crossed to Pseira for three days with twenty workmen. The results of these three days were such that it was decided to make Pseira the objective point of the work in 1907.

I was assisted by Mr. B. H. Berry, who remained through the season, and, in addition to the arduous work of making the plan and keeping an illustrated catalogue of the finds, was able to make some pen and ink sketches of the site, one of which is given in Plate II.

Work began on May 13th and continued until July 20th, making only about eight weeks of actual digging owing to the numerous interruptions caused by church holidays. The lack of water was our greatest difficulty, as it had to be brought by boat from springs on the mainland opposite. These springs, one at the Tholos of Kavousi, the other at the foot of some cliffs to the east, rise in holes dug in the sandy beaches, and in rough weather are entirely submerged. Except on one occasion we were able to keep at the excavations a sufficient supply for two days. Aside from this difficulty the men made themselves fairly comfortable in small bush huts, returning to their villages on Saturday nights to lay in their weekly stock of provisions. A small *quasi* cistern of the Roman period lying on the top of the point in the center of the excavations was converted into a temporary kitchen for our own use, tents having been brought over for sleeping purposes.

THE ISLAND.

The island of Pseira is a barren mass of rock rising from the sea at a point some two miles off the coast of Crete opposite the plain of Kavousi. Northwards from Pacheia Ammos a chain of rocky hills bounds the Kavousi valley on the west, descending in great cliffs into the Gulf of Mirabello. At the Tholos of Kavousi this chain, through some convulsion of nature, has been submerged; the isolated mass of Pseira, however, is beyond doubt a continuation of the same system, and rises abruptly from the sea on the western side. The position of the island is well shown in the sketch plan given in Vol. I, Part 1, page 9, of the *Transactions*.

The island measures some two miles north and south and at no point is more than a mile in width. The west coast is formed by a line of huge cliffs, which rise sheer from the sea to a height of 800 feet; on the east the land slopes sharply down to the shore. The eastern coast line is indented by three sandy coves separated from one another by tongues of land, the central one of which juts out into the sea for some two hundred yards. On the top and sides of this narrow point and on the adjoining hillside to the south once lay a flourishing Minoan settlement which evidently owed its existence to the excellent harborage for small craft offered by the sheltered cove on the south side of the point. It is exposed solely to the east, and an easterly gale is a thing of rare occurrence in Cretan waters (Plate III).

On the topmost ridge of the island on the edge of the high cliffs on the west lie the remains of a Roman military camp, probably a beacon station connected with similar posts at Kalo Khorio, Pacheia Ammos, the Tholos of Kavousi and on the island of Mochlos, which lies further to the east. Another small group of buildings occupies the center of the Minoan town on the long point before described, but owing to its limited area, this occupation did but little damage to the earlier structures.

Aside from the harbor the island could have offered but little to attract settlers of any sort even in Minoan days. Although numerous terrace walls show that the hillsides were once cultivated, the area was too small and the soil too scanty to attract an agricultural population. The Minoans were preeminently a maritime people, and all their settlements in Eastern Crete point to communities of traders and seamen rather than to a nation of husbandmen. On a coast affording so few places of refuge to sailing craft a good harbor was of primary importance to such settlers, and that the inhabitants of Minoan Pseira owed their extraordinary prosperity to their sheltered port seems very probable. Gournia, which had no harbor, never attained the same wealth or showed such signs of close intercourse with Knossos, the capital city of Crete, although it was probably the local seat of government. Even in the present day the port of the ancient Minoan town is constantly used in case of a sudden gale by the numerous sponge fishermen who work the Cretan waters on their way to and from the Libyan coast.

However much soil may have covered the rocky slopes of the island in Minoan times, in the 3,500 or more years which have passed since the destruction of the town the work of denudation has progressed to such an extent that the greater part of Pseira presents a bare and inhospitable surface. Except for an occasional herd of goats which are left there to feed during the winter months the island is absolutely deserted, and our arrival with eighty men is probably the largest invasion of its solitudes that has taken place since Roman times.

The water supply of the island seems to have been scanty. In the town itself no traces of wells or cisterns have as yet been found, a fact which would lead one to suppose that the townspeople were supplied by springs which have ceased to flow. A tradition exists among the country people on the opposite coast that there was once fresh water on Pseira, but in the present day the only supply is that held in a large cavity of natural rock close to the Roman ruins on the topmost ridge. This cavity is lined with Roman cement, but it must have furnished a precarious and inconvenient water supply, for in summer it would have been dry, and it lay at some distance from the town site. A single well, dating from the Roman or even an earlier period, has been found, sunk in the sand beach of a cove, a little to the north of the town site. It has walls of roughly dressed stones very like the Minoan house walls, and the water level is reached by a flight of eight steps formed of flat slabs. Owing to the general subsidence which is apparent on all this part of the coast, the sea has encroached so near to the well that the water is now brackish. Possibly this is the origin of the tradition about the presence of fresh water on the island. At any rate, the well must have remained open until fairly recent times. No objects have been found in the well itself, which can be assigned to pre-Roman times, but close to its mouth trial trenches have revealed parts of several Minoan houses of various periods and above them Roman remains showing that this cove was occupied in the same manner and at the same periods as the town site itself.

On the north side of the island the land is level but absolutely destitute of soil, and, as far as can be discovered, bears no traces of early occupation. On several parts of the south and east slopes sherds of Greek pottery, one of the late red-figured style, have been picked up, but so far no remains of a Greek building have come to light, although a thorough examination of the Roman buildings on the ridge and on the point may reveal the existence of Greek remains under their foundations.

A cemetery has been located on the southeast face of the island about half a mile from the town. Thirty-three graves have been opened, but the results are reserved for discussion in another place.

THE TOWN SITE.

The town of Pseira closely resembles the neighboring town excavated at Gournia, as will be seen by the plan (Plate I), but lies more picturesquely, a huddle of streets and houses along the top and sides of a rocky point with long flights of steps descending at irregular intervals to the water's edge. The small harbor lies on the south side of this point and here must have been the old landing place; from the head of this cove two main roads ascend, one on the left to the Late Minoan I houses on the south hill and the other on the right in a long stepway to the top of the rocky point which was the center of the town in all periods (Plate IV). Just below the summit of the hill this stepway branches into four, perhaps five, roads which traverse all parts of the flat hilltop. These roads along the level are never paved, but possess a more or less even floor of natural rock, whereas all the side alleys leading down to the sea have paved stepways, which are well preserved to-day.

The masonry is all of heavy, sometimes roughly squared blocks of stone, very strongly built in the style usually associated with the Late Minoan I period, but underlying these are many walls of the Middle Minoan I era. These walls are usually of lighter, smaller stones than those used in the upper stratum, although there is little or no means of separating the two periods by their wall construction.[1] There is no use of ashlar masonry on any part of the site and no house that can be compared to the Palace at Gournia, although three of the larger houses described below seem to have been those of important citizens. Unlike the corresponding settlements at Gournia and Vasiliki, bricks seem not to have been used in house construction, and the upper walls as well as many of the floors are entirely of stone. This fact may be the result of the difficulty in transporting bricks, which would necessarily have been brought from the mainland, but is also due, at least in part, to the abundance of excellent building material ready at hand and requiring but little labor. The island is composed in part of a hard gray limestone, stratified in many places close to the site, in thin layers with softer stone between, so that it can easily be broken off to form excellent building material for the walls of upper stories. For floors a soft slaty stone is used, which covers the hillside at the back of the town and splits into large slabs. In almost every house the upper floor is made of these slabs, which are always found blocking the basement rooms. In some cases, noticeably in the big house of H 12, Room 5 (see Plate I), these floors were still in their approximate positions, as apparently the basements had filled with rubbish before the

---

[1] Cf. the Early Minoan II and Middle Minoan I houses at Vasiliki, where the heavy outer walls and large bricks generally characteristic of the Late Minoan I period were used.

supporting beams of wood had rotted away, so that the upper floors, level with the thresholds of its rooms, were still clearly visible. Unfortunately the walls of this house, owing to the weight of the massive superstructure, were so thrown out of the perpendicular that all the upper courses had to be removed before the rooms could be cleared.

This universal use of stone accounts for the fragmentary condition of the pottery, of which unbroken specimens were very rare, as the falling in of stone floors and walls caused great destruction to everything except the heavier and coarser objects. The roads, in many places where the walls had fallen outwards, were blocked with masses of stones, the removal of which was the most serious difficulty encountered on the site. The earth, on the other hand, was easily disposed of, as from almost every house the dumping was over the cliffs into the sea below, and thus in two months we were able to clear the unusually large number of rooms shown on the plan.

In the trial dig of 1906 it was seen that Pseira was already a settlement of importance in the Middle Minoan I period; the later excavations have shown that the site was occupied as early as the Early Minoan II epoch. Owing to the uneven surface of the rock on which the earlier foundations were laid many relics of the first houses remained in the subsequent rebuildings of the Middle Minoan III and Late Minoan I periods, for in these rebuildings the walls were not always placed upon a rock foundation, but, where the surface of the natural rock was uneven, the fragments of earlier habitations were left in holes and crevices. The Early Minoan III and Middle Minoan I levels were everywhere closely connected, and in places it was hard to distinguish them. In fact, it would appear that no destruction and general rebuilding took place in these two periods and that one merged gradually into the other with no distinct line of demarcation.

Under the floors of Late Minoan I and Middle Minoan III houses there was in many cases a deposit of Middle Minoan I sherds associated with house walls, and, in these same houses, directly underlying the Middle Minoan I deposits, sometimes mixed with them, were fragments of Early Minoan III vases. From this it would appear that the people of the Middle Minoan I period still used the houses of the preceding period, but usually formed a new floor at a slightly higher level. This close connection between these early periods confirms the belief that they extended over no great space of years; in the Early Minoan II period one already finds the beginnings of a light on dark style of pottery, which is the prevailing Early Minoan III ware and the forerunner of the polychrome vases of the Middle Minoan I period.

The exact extent of the town in the Middle Minoan I era is doubtful, but that it was confined to the point and did not cover its entire area seems probable, as no sherds of the early periods have been found on the south hill or on the north side of the point except at one place in K 11, where a few sherds and a hoard of obsidian flakes and cores indicated the site of an Early Minoan II or possibly an Early Minoan I building. The place was destroyed in the Middle Minoan I period and not rebuilt until the Middle Minoan III period, when the era of its greatest prosperity began, an era which was continued without interruption until the town was overtaken by the same general catastrophe which destroyed all the settlements in this part of Crete. Unlike Gournia and Palaiokastro, it never recovered from this blow, and after the end of the Late Minoan I period was apparently deserted.

Although the stratification of the earlier periods is interesting, as it confirms the conclusions drawn from other sites, it is to the Late Minoan I period that we must turn for the bulk of the finds and the best preserved houses. On all sites the period of destruction is the one which leaves the richest harvest for the excavator. As long as a site is in continuous occupation the earlier deposits are only the refuse of breakage and objects which have ceased to be of service to their owners. They are thrown into rubbish heaps and used as artificial fillings to make even floors over naturally uneven surfaces. Where, as at Pseira, the town was destroyed in the height of its prosperity with no extensive later settlements to disturb its ruins the finds are of course unusually rich. If the town had come to an end with its first destruction in the Middle Minoan I era the same would have been the case with the remains of that period, but, as we have seen, the rebuilding which took place in the Middle Minoan III and Late Minoan I periods destroyed nearly all that remained of the earlier houses. From the end of the Late Minoan I era, however, to which period must be assigned the final catastrophe, no settlers appeared on the site until Roman times, and even then in very small numbers. Their houses occupied a space some 20 by 30 metres square on the top of the point, and probably destroyed only two or three houses of the earlier period.

The Late Minoan I town had increased considerably in size and the overcrowding of the point caused the formation of a new quarter on the hill to the south of the cove, nearly doubling the original area of habitation. The streets, long stepways and heavy well built house walls belong to this period of expansion which came to an untimely end in one of the first upheavals that eventually involved the overthrow of the Cretan maritime supremacy in the Aegean. This uneasy period of invasions and wars of which these destructions of East Cretan towns are the precursors eventually brought about the sack of Knossos, the capital city, and thus dealt a death blow to the Minoan kingdom as a united whole. It is not yet clear whether this was caused by internal wars or by the pressure of the wild tribes of the north, but the fact that these small islands were not resettled shows that the loss of maritime power rendered them unsafe and open to attack by sea. While Crete still held the control of the Aegean a small island like Pseira was safe enough, and that such a settlement could attain the prosperity shown by the masses of stone vases, the big painted jars (Pl. VII) and the plaster relief (Pl. V) proves that the people of the Late Minoan I period lived in a state of peace and security utterly unprepared to withstand an armed foe. Once the blow had fallen and the sea power was overthrown a small island was too precarious a place for a town, and the survivors of the catastrophe took refuge in some of the neighboring coast settlements which partially recovered their prosperity. On the mainland in case of attack the people could seek refuge in the hills, but on Pseira their only means of flight was by sea, and even this was impossible without long warning of the enemy's approach.

The painted plaster relief and the big painted jars of the "Palace Style" show not only a prosperous community, but one enjoying close communication with Knossos. Moreover, it is important to note that Knossian products are found in contexts which would otherwise have been thought earlier; in other words, Late Minoan II Palace style vases are found in Late Minoan I deposits. Now it is certain that Pseira was never occupied in the Late Minoan II period; accordingly these vases must have been made where the Palace style had already attained a foothold. This would naturally have been Knossos, where this ware first appeared at the end of the Late Minoan I period and soon attained great popularity. Thus while the towns in the east of Crete were still making ware of the Late Minoan I style, stray vases of this later technique had already begun to find their way from Knossos to these remote settlements. No doubt had the destruction occurred a few years later or had there been an immediate resettlement of the town, the Palace style would have been found the prevailing ware as at Palaiokastro, where such a resettlement actually took place and where the Late Minoan II Palace style can be said to represent a distinct period. On the isthmus, however, the disaster was of too overwhelming a nature to allow an immediate revival, and even at Gournia there was no Late Minoan II period, the rebuilding of the west slope taking place in the Late Minoan III epoch, after the Palace style had degenerated into a highly conventional form. The few Palace style vases from Gournia are, as at Pseira, either foreign to the site or at most an attempt by the local potter to copy designs that he had seen elsewhere. In speaking, then, of the Late Minoan I period at Pseira we must consider that it probably overlaps the Late Minoan II period of Knossos and that the Late Minoan I pottery persisted for a longer time on these small sites than it did at the artistic headquarters of the kingdom, where the new styles must naturally have originated.

THE HOUSES.

Turning to the left from the head of the main stepway in H 8 (see plan), we reach the house in I 5, which is of peculiar interest, as it reproduces on a small scale many of the features of Knossian architecture.

Crossing the threshold, a narrow passage (1) leads into an open space (3). From here one enters a small megaron (2) through a triple doorway supported on two stone bases with the dowel holes for fastening the wooden door posts. In one corner of this megaron is a small rectangular construction divided from the main room by a low partition of upright slabs of greenish schist. A round outlet hole in the paved floor which shows traces of a plaster coating makes it probable that we have here a small bath. As the swallow hole is so large that it was hardly meant to be plugged, the bath was probably never filled, but contained an earthenware vessel from which the water could be poured over the bather. Between this bath and the south wall of the megaron a double door with a stone base for the central post leads into a passage also connecting with the main entrance of the house. Behind the bath a small stone stair leads toward an upper floor which must have contained the principal living rooms. This house is one of the latest additions to the town just before its destruction and belongs to the period when the Palace style of pottery of Knossos was just reaching Eastern Crete, as is shown by fragments of a small jug of this class of imported ware.

Farther along the unexcavated road on which lies the house just described is found another house in J 3. It lies on the summit of the knoll, with rooms terraced down the hill on both sides. It is of the usual type, but peculiar, inasmuch as it overlies a more ancient building, three rooms of which, 1, 2 and 3, were filled with masses of round beach pebbles. This deposit was about 50 centimeters deep and must have been much greater originally, as in building the later house the upper layers had been cut away. The workmen at once recognized these pebbles as sling stones, and it is probable that this was really their use and that the building was a kind of primitive arsenal.[1]

Turning down the small alley behind the house with the bath we reach another narrow stepway which leads down to a lower roadway running along the side of the ravine north and south. In G 5 this road crossed the torrent bed to the south hill, where a large part of it has been carried away. All the houses in G. H. 3-7 open on this roadway, and among them one is

---

[1] I am indebted to Dr. Georg Karo for calling my attention to the fact that Mr. Tsountas in his excavations in the Cyclades found round towers filled with similar pebbles which he also considers sling stones (Tsountas, Ἐφ. Ἀρχ. 1899, p. 120). That such weapons were used is shown in the siege scene on the silver vase-fragment from Mycenae (Tsountas and Manatt, The Mycenean Age, p. 213).

especially noticeable for its massive outer walls and huge threshold. In this house, H 4, there were only two narrow basements on the road level (1, 2). Their back walls were formed by a ledge of natural rock, which with the heavy street wall supported the rooms of the upper floor. To these a stone stair ascended from the paved entrance hall, but as the soil at this point was very shallow little could be learned as to size or plan of these upper rooms except that they could also be reached from the back, where a second entrance connected them with the narrow stepway mentioned above.

The only objects found lay in the basements 1 and 2, into which they had fallen when the upper floors gave way. A jar from this hoard shown in Fig. 13, is a good specimen of the local Late Minoan I ware in Eastern Crete. Jars of this sort were very common at Pseira, and several were also found at Gournia. The work as a rule is coarse and the execution of the design careless. White paint for details and added red bands are very noticeable on jars of this class, which, though far from beautiful, hold the eye by their bold design.

The most remarkable features of the domestic architecture of the houses on Pseira are the interior staircases of stone, found in almost every house and best shown in these houses along the south slope. The steepness of the hill and the fact that the light walls of the smaller houses were not strong enough to support a heavy superstructure caused each house to be built in terraces connected by stone stairs leading from one tier of rooms to those on the higher level. Thus a single house would contain a number of floors yet never stand more than two stories high at any one point. Such houses are well shown in the siege scene on the silver vase-fragment from Mycenae; in fact, they can be found to-day in Cretan hill villages which closely resemble in construction their predecessors of Minoan times. In some cases, where the outer walls are built of unusually heavy stones, the superstructure may have been higher, but the general type was a large house climbing the hillside with not more than one floor of living rooms over the basements of each tier.

Returning once more to the head of the main stepway in H 8, which, oddly enough, has no house opening into it from top to bottom, we find the first road on the right leading into the middle of a large building with no distinct threshold or entrance hall. The rooms of this house, which I have called House A, are all of large size, and the presence of a column base in R. 5, very heavy buttresses and thick walls show it possessed important upper floors which opened on another roadway in H 10 at a higher level.

The south part of this house which lies on the edge of the cliff has been broken away, so that its exact extent cannot be determined; moreover, the shallow soil of the upper tier has obliterated all traces of the rooms in that direction. Scattered along the lower road and evidently dropped by plunderers lay five stone vases which speak for the original contents of the house. In quality of stone and finish they are excelled by no other finds of the season, and although little else was found in the house, they show that it must have belonged to a wealthy citizen (Fig. 15 *l m*). This house is rivaled in point of size by only one other (House B in H 12), and both of them are much larger than any of the houses at Gournia excepting, of course, the small palace at that site. This may be explained by saying that Gournia was the seat of the local governor of this part of the ancient Minoan kingdom, although the small town of Pseira was the more prosperous of the two. Gournia would certainly have been the more suitable residence for the local official, as it lay on the mainland in what was a populous district in Minoan times, if we may judge from the many remains of that period in the immediate neighborhood.

The second road on the right from the head of the main stepway has not been entirely cleared, but it is plain that just before reaching the entrance of the above mentioned house a branch leads east from it while the main part descends at a slight angle to H 11, where it turns sharply down the hill in a broad stepway paved with massive slabs. At the top of this stepway to the east a very large threshold leads into House B, the largest cleared thus far on the island. Like House A, this appears to have been merely the house of a wealthy citizen, and in plan and construction differs in no way from its humbler neighbors. Its large size and important upper floors required massive walls of large stones, which in some places were preserved to a height of three metres. Like the smaller houses, this also climbed the hill in tiers, of which we can count four reaching from the water's edge to the summit of the point.

The outer wall facing the road is built of roughly squared blocks of stone approaching ashlar masonry. From the threshold one enters a paved ante-room or entrance hall (2), and this connects in turn with the rooms lying over the deep basements of the second tier (5, 7). From the north side of this entrance hall a narrow stone stair ascends to the third tier of rooms, in only one of which (4) were any objects found. From room No. 3 of this tier another stair leads to the rooms of the fourth and last tier lying on the actual hilltop, but the soil at this point was so shallow and had been so disturbed in Roman times that no trace of their plan remains. The first tier, close to the water's edge, was also very much destroyed, and its walls were so thrown out of perpendicular by the weight of earth above that the few that remained collapsed as soon as cleared. Like the entrance hall, the rooms on the same level with it over the basements of the second tier were all paved with large slabs, some nearly a metre square. In Room 5 this paved floor was still in its approximate position, the basement having filled with debris before the supports of the upper floor had given way.

From various parts of this house came the best finds of the season, chiefly of vases and stone lamps, but, judging from the fragments scattered about the rooms, they represented but a small part of its original contents. The road outside the main entrance was filled with hundreds of fragments of fine painted cups and vases, which seemed to have been thrown out at the time the place was sacked. This sack must have been carried out thoroughly, as no metal or any small portable objects were left behind. The pottery seemed to have been wantonly destroyed; parts of the same vase were found scattered through various rooms of the house as though they had been broken and then kicked about the floors. Parts of the stone lamp (Fig. 19) were found in Rooms 4, 5 and 7, while the bottle in Fig. 8 came from Rooms 7, 8 and 9.

On the north side of the hilltop in J, K, 11-15, were a number of rooms which belonged to a row of houses standing along the edge of the cliffs. The easternmost of these houses are not clearly distinguishable one from another owing to Roman foundation walls which were sunk into their deposits and also to the fact that the greater part of each house, because of the corrosion of the cliffs, has slipped into the sea.

In J 13 we find the probable continuation of one of the roads starting east from the head of the main stepway so often referred to. Immediately on the left of this road lie the walls of a small but well built house, J, K, 12. The main entrance leading into R. 4 is reached from a small alley which turns off the main road on the left. Room 4 lay on the upper floor over a low basement, and owing to the sharp slope of the ground at this point is on the same level as the ground floor room or court marked No. 1, which lies higher up the hillside. Room 1 seems to have been a small paved court with a sort of portico across the north side which led to the rooms entered from the street 2 and 4. In the narrow portico, evidently fallen from an upper floor, were parts of a plaster relief representing a Minoan queen or goddess in a richly embroidered dress. Because of the shallow soil at this point the surviving fragments were very rotten, and only those in fullest relief had withstood the action of time. These include one breast, arms and part of the skirt, which are shown in Pl. V, where a conjectural restoration of the bust has been attempted. Aside from this relief the house was a singularly empty one, probably because it was more carefully plundered than its neighbors. The few potsherds found all belong to the Late Minoan I period, which lingered on here after the Late Minoan II Palace style, with its great frescoes and reliefs, had already commenced at Knossos.

Further along the ridge in I, 14, 15 another large house (D) has been partially cleared. In size it rivals the two neighboring houses already described, and, judging from the objects found, was an equally rich one. The heavy walls and massive buttresses again indicate important upper floors. One of the basements, 2, was lighted by a window and used as a storeroom. Both

2 and 5 have paved floors and connect with the rooms behind by a doorway. In 5 nine large jars were found standing in a row along the south wall of the room on each side of the doorway. All except two were painted with bands of poor dark paint, but these two belong to a very different class. One is shown in Fig. 9 and the other is quite like it except for a difference in the rim. It is hard to explain the presence of such jars in a narrow dark store-room, where the plain unpainted jar would have fulfilled the same purpose. Possibly they were hidden there among the others on the chance that they might be overlooked by the spoilers.

Apparently these rooms, 2, 3, 5, were the result of a rebuilding of this part of the house on a more regular plan, as the very irregular range of rooms in I 15 belongs to the same building. In a corner of 1 is a curious semicircular construction of solid masonry exactly similar to one found in a room of the Palace at Gournia. At about 1.50 m. from the ground the outer circle of masonry ends, making a shelf about .30 m. broad, while the central core rises about .30 m. higher, making a second shelf or platform in the corner. From its resemblance to the fireplaces seen to-day in many of the Cretan inns, this was probably its use, although no traces of fire were found.

Of the other houses which lie still farther along the point little can be said except that they repeat the usual features of these small Minoan dwellings and contained no objects of especial interest.

In I 16 two more roads were found leading up towards the summit of the hill, and it is clear that the houses extended to the very end of the point, which has evidently subsided to a considerable degree. Many of the houses are now drenched by spray in a heavy storm, and others still lower on the rock at the end of the point have been almost completely swept away by the action of the waves.

THE POTTERY.

THE EARLY MINOAN PERIOD.

EARLY MINOAN I.

Of the Early Minoan I period there are no traces on the point excepting a large hoard of obsidian cores and flakes associated with early potsherds in K 11, R. 1. These sherds are of coarse gritty clay, black or brown, and very highly burnished. One piece of a cover and a cup with suspension handles have a very early look, although they might equally well belong to the first part of the succeeding period.

EARLY MINOAN II.

Almost all the rock crevices on the hill were filled with fragments of this period, both the mottled red and black and the dark on light geometric techniques being represented. Under the floor of Room 4 in House A a large deposit of this period came to light, including a perfect jug of the mottled style and a side-spouted jar of the common Vasiliki type (*Trans.*, Vol. I, Part III, Pl. XXXIV, Nos. 6 and 7), with a geometrical design in white, showing the influence of the succeeding period. The wares of this period are not essentially different from those found at Vasiliki in 1904 and 1906, and as no new shapes or styles occurred, they do not require any further description.

The stratification, where it could be recognized, carried out what had already been noted at Vasiliki and elsewhere, that the dark on light geometric ware lay immediately beneath the light on dark Early Minoan III pottery, while the mottled technique was found in both deposits, though to a far lesser degree in the latter.

EARLY MINOAN III.

The town which occupied a small area during the preceding period now attained considerable size. The principal deposits of this ware came from rock crevices under the Late Minoan I floors in G 6 and on the summit of

   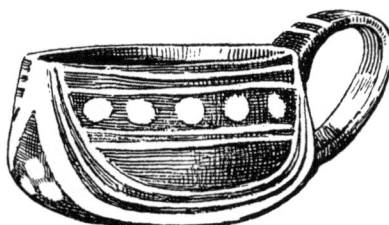

Fig. 1.   Fig. 2.

the point H. 4, where the Later Minoan I walls did not reach the underlying strata owing to the depth of soil. No remains of this period have as yet been found under the Late Minoan I houses on the south hill.

Judging from the masses of sherds in some of the rock holes this period was a long one, merging gradually into the Middle Minoan I period with no distinct line of separation such as marks the end of the Middle Minoan I and Late Minoan I periods on this site. In many cases the Early Minoan III and Middle Minoan I deposits were very much confused, and a certain type of cup (Figs. 1 and 2) seemed to form a connecting link between the two and occurred with the remains of both periods. This type did not appear in the Early Minoan III deposits of Vasiliki, where decorated cups of this shape were always without handles, but was found at Palaiokastro (*B. S. A.* XI, p. 271, Fig. 5d), in Middle Minoan I deposits; moreover, several undecorated cups of this type came from the Middle Minoan I house B at Vasiliki. On the other hand, this same type occurred in several undoubtedly Early Minoan III graves in the cemetery. These cups are occasionally decorated with a festoon in red paint, thus foreshadowing the Middle Minoan I polychrome style. The appearance of this type of cup in both periods emphasizes the close connection between them uninterrupted by any overwhelming disaster.

THE MIDDLE MINOAN PERIOD.

MIDDLE MINOAN I.

The soil in I 6 was unusually deep owing to the gradual slope of the hill at this point, and it was soon evident that the Late Minoan I floors were not laid on a rock foundation. Below these floors the walls of

Fig. 3.

an earlier Middle Minoan I house were found. It was orientated like the later house, and in many cases the Late Minoan I walls were laid on the top of those of the earlier building. Unfortunately at certain points this was not the case, and the Late Minoan I builders had sunk their foundations deep into the Middle Minoan I deposits. Owing to this fact almost no objects were found entire, but that the original house would have proved a rich one was shown by the parts of nine stone vases and many more in clay. Three of the stone vases were found entire, one of which is shown in Fig. 15, and is a typical example of the low open bowl so much in vogue in this period.

The other fragmentary vases were, with one exception, parts of similar bowls of various sizes, the exception being a cup in fine gray veined limestone with a trefoil spout. More important is the jug shown in Fig. 3. Its uptilted spout recalls some of the Early Minoan III shapes and the white design on a dark ground shows the simple beginnings of a curvilinear style but little removed from the methods of Early Minoan III decoration.

Together with this jug were several large jars and covers representing the Middle Minoan I dark on light style, which was commonly used for all the larger, coarser vessels. This ware, three examples of which are shown in Fig. 4, is always characterized by its buff clay and bold designs in slightly lustrous dark paint. The clay in the larger vessels is generally coarse, but in the small vases the designs are painted on a smooth buff slip which sometimes shows signs of polishing. The favorite designs are parallel sets of oblique lines running from the neck to the base of the vase, large scrolls like a running spiral pattern with the spirals filled in, and rectilinear designs

Fig. 4.

like those on the vases of this class found at Vasiliki (*Trans.*, II, 2, p. 128, Figs. 11 and 12.

Some of the smaller vases with the polished buff slip and geometrical dark on light designs closely resemble the ware in use at the beginning of the Early Minoan II period, when the mottled technique is still in its earliest stages. The cups shown in Plate VI *a* and *b* came from H. 3, R. 3, and belong to this class except that here we have an added white paint, so combining both the dark on light and light on dark styles. The thinness and fine quality of the clay is very unusual in the dark on light wares of this period and shows that this style of decoration was sometimes used for vases of the better class. The other vessels from this deposit included a number of black glaze cups with festoons of white paint on the rim like those which characterized House B. at Vasiliki and which have also been found at Palaiokastro in the same context; also a small black glaze cup with a white fish, a design common in this period. (*Trans.*, Vol. I, Part III, p. 189, Fig. 6, IIe.) (*Id.*, II, 2, Pl. XXX *b*.)

Under the Late Minoan I floor in G. 7, R. 2, was found the curious vase shown in Fig. 5. As the deposit was characterized by masses of

Middle Minoan I cup fragments, there can be no doubt but that this vase belonged to the same period. The exaggerated shape and the large size of the vessel show that the Middle Minoan I era was by no means a primitive period and that no great transition was required to produce the exquisite polychrome pottery of Knossos with their curious shapes. In the case of this vase the shape was the principal consideration, and to emphasize it no decoration which could distract the eye was employed, half the body being painted with chalky white, the other half black. That the shape was derived from a metal prototype is shown by the clay rivet on the vertical handle, and though a metal vase of this shape may have had an especial use, its copy in clay was hardly practical but merely an example of the potter's skill.

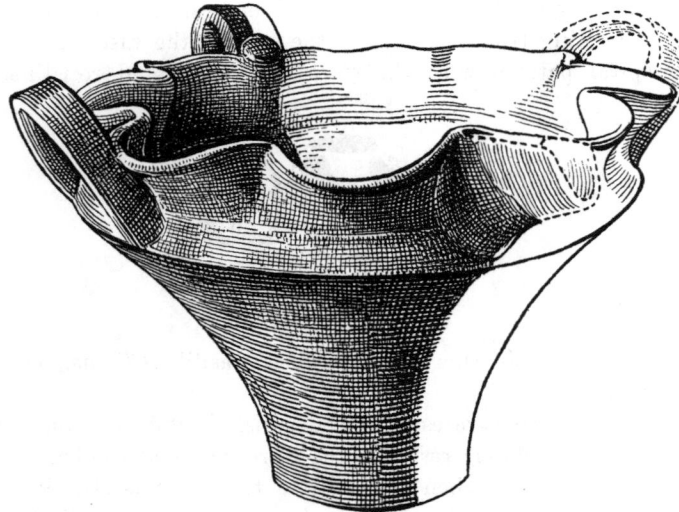

Fig. 5.

MIDDLE MINOAN III.

That the resettlement of the island took place near the end of the Middle Minoan period seems clear from extensive rubbish heaps found among the Late Minoan I houses of a kind of ware which immediately precedes the typical Late Minoan I style of pottery. This ware is of very fine quality and in it we see that the dark on light designs of the succeeding period already predominate over the old Middle Minoan I light on dark style. The light on dark technique is in a decided minority and consists usually of a monochrome white design on a dark ground. The dark on light style is confined almost entirely to variations of the ripple motive, with no sign of the naturalistic plant designs so much in vogue in the Middle Minoan III and Late Minoan I periods. The vases are usually hole-mouthed jugs and low open bowls, the latter of which commonly have the ripple both inside and out, also a similar style made of broad wavy brush marks. White paint is sometimes used for details on broad dark bands, but there is no trace of the Late Minoan I red. This style of pottery may be said to occupy an intermediate stage between the true Middle Minoan III ware of Knossos and the typical Late Minoan I fabrics, and cannot truly be said to belong to either class. As true Middle Minoan III pottery has not been found so far on any of the sites in this neighborhood, I have called this ware by that name to distinguish it from the later Late Minoan I wares of which it is the forerunner. The deposits of this style were all very fragmentary, no vases entire and none that could be made up from fragments. The evidence shows that it was a period of resettlement and merged into the Late Minoan I period very shortly afterwards, when the town was entirely rebuilt.

THE LATE MINOAN PERIOD.

LATE MINOAN I.

The Late Minoan I local pottery of Pseira presents much the same characteristics as that of Gournia, which is to say the prevailing designs are drawn from plant life or from marine objects. The ripple design, which, as I have said, attained such great popularity in the Middle Minoan III period, did not easily die out, and on some of the best Late Minoan I vases we find it occurring combined with designs typical of that period (Fig. 6). The use of white paint for details begins at the end of the Middle Minoan III period and later a chalky red is introduced for the same purpose. The monochrome light on dark Middle Minoan III style persists in many black glaze cups with a design in white around the rim. Of these cups the commonest type is straight sided with a slightly flaring rim encircled by a band of very stiff and regular white spirals.[1]

For the Middle Minoan III ripple vases a very fine buff slip had been revived, which recalls the polished buff slips of Early Minoan II and Middle Minoan I vases, except that the new slip possessed a harder surface and presented a more brilliant appearance. The use of the slip increased to such an extent in the Late Minoan I period that it is unusual to find a decorated vase without it. The paint used is in itself very lustrous and when combined with the polished slip gives to the surface of the Late Minoan I vases, where well preserved, a finish unequaled by the ware of any of

---

[1] Cf. *Gournia*, Plate VI, Fig. 35.

the preceding periods. On all large jars which are of coarse gritty clay this slip was valuable to give a smooth surface for the painted design, although it was not universally used, for a thin buff wash was sometimes substituted. The jars with this buff wash are always of an inferior sort, decorated with either plain bands or coarse plant designs in very lustrous paint.

Another type is occasionally found which recalls the Middle Minoan I period and in a lesser degree the polished dark subneolithic ware of Early

Fig. 6.

Minoan II. These are cups and jugs of dark gray clay of fine quality covered with a shiny black varnish which peels away from the surface very easily. This is an archaistic revival of an older style and is sometimes noticed in Middle Minoan I vases, although it does not appear to have ever become popular, judging from the few examples found. Small jars were very frequently found with crude flowers, usually a lily, incised when the clay was still moist in place of a painted design.

Another archaism is found on several clay bulls from the town, which are covered with a chalky white slip, over which is painted a harness in either an orange red or purple (Fig. 7). This technique occurs occasionally in the Middle Minoan I period, but in the Late Minoan I period was probably confined to these bulls; at least I do not know of its use on any vases of the period. That a white bull was the favorite sacrificial victim seems clear, and the custom that the votive-offering should also be white necessitated the use of this otherwise uncommon white slip.

One of the most curious facts about the finds of this period was the widely scattered condition of broken objects. In many cases broken vases and stone

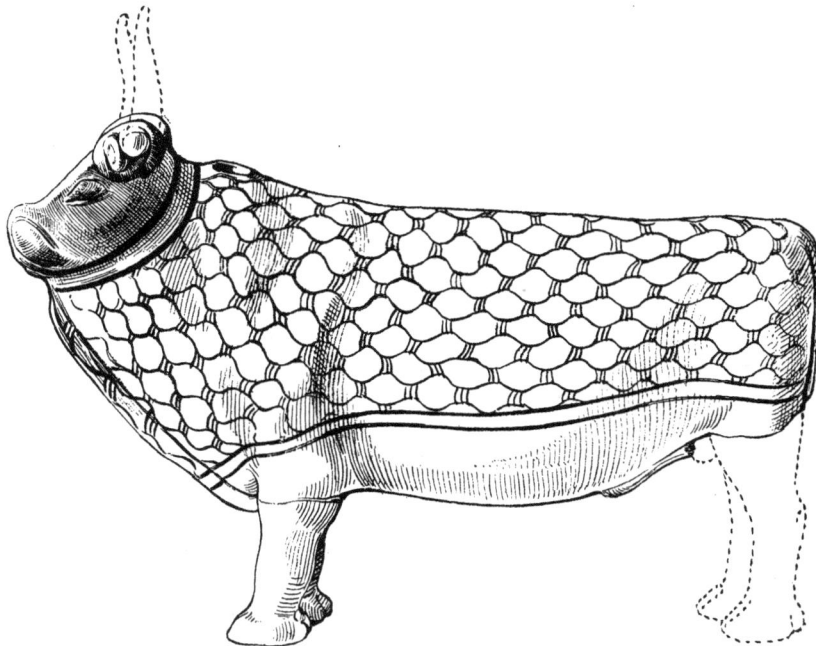

Fig. 7.

vessels were found piece by piece in various rooms of the same house and sometimes scattered over even a larger area. One small lamp (Fig. 18) was found in H. 12, R. 8, early in the season, and on the last day its handle turned up in I. 14, R. 5. When we remember that the upper walls of most of the houses were of stone as well as their floors, this is not so surprising, as the destruction probably left many houses standing in a partly ruined condition and accessible to any wanderers who might return to the site. Thus in many cases parts of a vase may have· been picked up, carried a little distance and dropped again if something else was found of greater value. Clay vases, as we have said, must have been knocked off from shelves when the house was sacked and their fragments scattered about the rooms as too bulky and worthless a form of plunder. The sack, combined with the falling in of so many stone walls and floors, left very few vases entire, although the large jars, which were heavy and not easily overturned, were unusually complete.

As is always the case on these town sites, many houses were entirely empty, and the finds of clay vases came from certain large deposits which by some chance escaped utter destruction. Dealing with these deposits first, there are in all fifteen vases, for the most part cups and bowls, which come from D. 5, R. 1, a new house of which only part of one room has been opened up. This room was filled with thousands of finely decorated Late Minoan I sherds, from which the above mentioned vases were put together. Twelve baskets of painted potsherds and as many again of coarser vessels represent the breakage of an enormous mass of pottery which must have formed the stock of a dealer. These vases, though good examples of their class, present no new features, the designs being for the most part plant wreaths and similar motives.

The next deposit in House A. would seem to have fallen into a basement room under the entrance hall, where we find the threshold opening off the upper road—H. 10, R. 1. The two best vases from this deposit are shown in Fig. 6 and Pl. VI c. One, the tall amphora (Fig. 6) with the ripple and plant motives, is a shape more characteristic of the preceding than of the Late Minoan I period, but the designs and the use of white paint for the details show it must be classed early in this period. The other vase (Pl. VI c) is a very good example of the Late Minoan I style at its best. The influence of the Middle Minoan light on dark technique is still very strong, as shown by the ivy pattern in white on the central band, while the ivy leaves with spiral volutes are very typical of the period to which the vase belongs. A clay bull similar to the one in Fig. 7 was found with the vases and is painted in a way already described, with an orange harness over the white body slip. Three such bulls were found entire or nearly so, also parts of three others. All but one of these bulls appear to have been made from the same mould, probably turned out by the local potter for votive-offerings, or, as Mr. Dawkins suggests (*B. S. A.*, Vol. XI, p. 287), as a cheap substitute for sacrifice used by the townspeople in their religious ceremonies. It seems probable that each household had its own little shrine, for Gournia is the only place where a town shrine has been discovered. In the poorer houses these shrines must have been of the simplest type with accessory cult objects of a perishable character, but in houses of the better class on several sites what appear to have been the remains of domestic shrines have been found (*B. S. A.*, Vol. X, p. 216).[2] In House B. R. 4 parts of a

---

[2] At Palaikastro there seems to have been a Minoan shrine on the site of the later temple of Dictean Zeus which may be a town shrine such as the one at Gournia (*B. S. A.*, Vol. XI, p. 287).

large clay bull's head were found and nearby a narrow ledge of small beach pebbles which may have served such a use, as the late shrine in the palace of

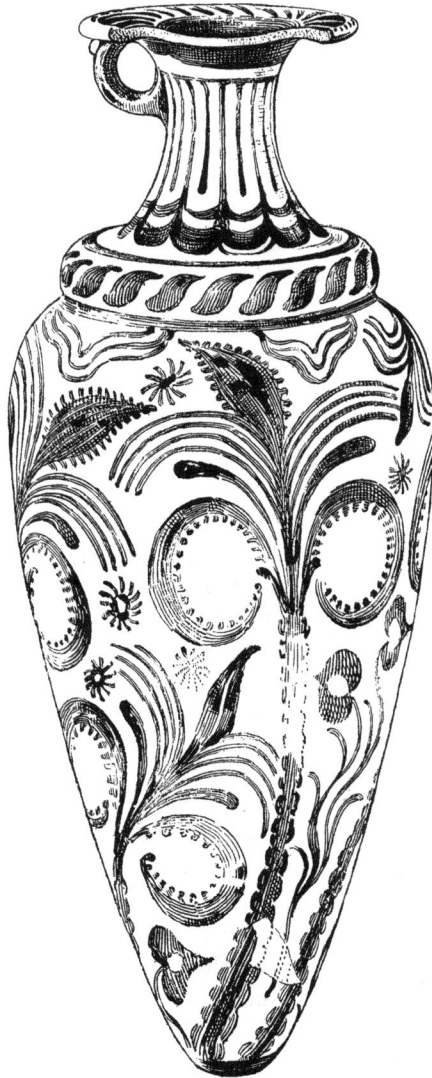

Fig. 8.

Knossos shows that such beach pebbles were employed for altars. Near this ledge was found a triton shell cut out inside to form a vessel, and this again recalls a Knossian shrine, for in the Middle Minoan III shrine of the Snake Goddess shells were associated with cult objects. At Pseira a number of such shells have been found, in different houses, usually cut out inside in the way just described, and evidence points to the fact that shells of all sorts were associated in some way with Minoan ritual.

To return to the pottery once more, some of the best finds of the year were made in House B. and in every case had fallen into the deep basements from the rooms of the upper floors. The flask or filler of Fig. 8 comes from this house and is one of the class of vessels showing strong influences of the Late Minoan II Palace style. The motive is evidently that of the date palm, and although the stiff architectural style of the full Palace period is lacking, it needs only a step, and an easy one at that, to produce the splendid Palace style jars of Knossos with the lotus and papyrus designs. The design on the neck is quite unlike the true Late Minoan I style; moreover, this shape of bottle filler seems not to have made its appearance until the end of the Late Minoan I period, when it attains popularity almost to the exclusion of the conical straight sided filler. This straight sided shape survives in the Late Minoan III period after the bottle style has disappeared with the end of the Late Minoan II pottery.

The only other vase from this house (R. 1) which is in any way remarkable is the large jar shown in Plate VII, which is, without doubt, one of the finest examples of the Late Minoan I period that has been found thus far in Crete. The profuse use of white paint for the details, the presence of chalky red band on the rim prove that it belongs to the Late Minoan I style at the last stage of its development. The design of bulls' heads and double axes is itself conventionally treated, but such designs in which sacred emblems play an important part do not lend themselves easily to naturalistic treatment. It is in the olive sprays that fill the spaces between the stiff heads that we see the love of naturalism which characterizes the artist of this period, and in this case they help to lighten the heaviness of the whole design. The lower zones of decoration are splendid examples of the various types of spirals, ivy leaves and plant rosettes with which the Late Minoan I potters loved to cover their vases, and which one meets again and again on every class of ware from the end of the Middle Minoan III to the beginning of the Late Minoan II period. From the profuse use of the double axe motive it is probable that this jar was reserved for some ritual use. The double axe appears on the top and sides of the rim, on the shoulder between the horns and heads of the bulls, and on the base, and even the handles take their form from the same cult object. The large axes on the shoulder bear on their blades the same designs worked in white paint that occur so often on the axes figured on seal stones and in scenes of ritual worship, and must be taken to represent the actual manner in which the original objects themselves were decorated. It is possible that these details in white may stand for the exact reproductions in a paint medium of metal axes inlaid with silver wire, an art not unknown to the Minoan goldsmiths. The rim is very deeply undercut and pierced with a row of small holes through which a coarse needle could be passed to sew on cloth covering over the top of the jar, so as to exclude all dust from defiling the contents. It may be that the jar was used for holding oil or some other liquid sacred to the gods, in which case this cover would keep the contents pure, whereas an earthenware cover would never fit closely enough to exclude dust from sifting in. The splendid results obtained by the Late Minoan I polished slip are well shown here where the rather coarse clay is covered by a heavy coat of finer clay so polished that no sign is visible of the rough material of which the vase is formed. The bulls' heads are painted in dark glaze with harness of white, which rather contradicts the theory that the bull most acceptable to the divinities should be white, but in this case a white head on the light buff slip would have been nearly invisible, and a light design on a light ground would, as far as we know, have been contrary to all Minoan traditions of vase painting. The white harness is also a divergence from the usual harness of orange red, but it seems that here the exigencies of the case obliged the artist to adopt new methods more suitable to his background on which his designs must of necessity be in dark glaze. With this vase we reach the highest stage of development in Late Minoan I ceramic art, which in point of paint, glaze and slip is unsurpassed by either earlier or later wares in Minoan Crete.

The bull's head before mentioned came also from this house, but, unfortunately, the greater part of it is missing. This head is rather larger than those from other sites and has the greater part of one of the horns intact, which, as a rule, are lacking on the other heads. Like the clay bulls from other parts of the site, it is covered with a chalky white slip. The closed neck shows that it was never attached to a body.

The next vase deposit to be described was found in House D, in the two basement rooms 2 and 5. In R. 5, among a number of small pithoi, was found the jar of Fig. 9. Another larger one, an exact duplicate except for the rim, was found with it, and seemed to have been filled with some very fine plaster. These two jars were standing, as stated above, p. 14, together with seven coarser ones of a very inferior quality. Their original use must have been a purely decorative one, as their very slender base and heavy rim render them a very unsafe receptacle for any material.

The most curious feature of the jar in Fig. 9 is the moulded rim. Dr. Mackenzie tells me that fragments of such rims have been found at Knossos, and I believe they have appeared at Phaistos also; but no one has had any very clear idea as to what sort of vessels they came from. The body is of coarse clay covered with the usual polished buff slip, except around the rim, where the same chalky white already noticed on the bulls has been employed.

Fig. 9.

The whole body of the jar except for a zone near the base is covered with a network of connected spirals in dark glaze picked out with white dots. The lower zone, separated from the rest by dark bands, is decorated with a row of loose spirals. The background is filled in with dark glaze, leaving the pattern in the natural buff of the clay, a method new to these sites on the isthmus. The

Fig. 10.

network of spirals forcibly recalls certain architectural designs, and is in all probability a potter's adaptation of designs from the walls and ceilings of the great Minoan palaces. The jar has the look of having been copied from a metal original, and one can well imagine such a metal jar with the curious rim and spiral net in repoussée, the white dots inlaid with silver.

In G. 7, R. 1, which was cleared in the three days' trial made on the site in 1906, were found a splendid set of vases, three of which are shown in Figs. 10 and 11 and 12. Like the flask of Fig. 8 they might be classed as Late Minoan II were it not for the undoubted Late Minoan I character of all the objects associated with them. The flask or bottle filler with the dolphins, Fig. 10, was found lying partly inside one of the earlier conical fillers of which Gournia furnished such fine specimens in 1903. The old Middle Minoan I design of the fish again appears here, but the treatment is now rather more realistic, as the dolphins in this case are enmeshed in a net which covers the body of the vase. The design at once recalls the large fresco of dolphins from Knossos, so that again, as in the jar of Fig. 9, we find the potters copying designs from the walls of the Cretan palaces—in this case not so well adapted to their humble craft.

Fig. 11.

The jar in Fig. 11 looks as though it belonged to the end of the Late Minoan II rather than to the end of the Late Minoan I period, the small barred stop-gaps between the curls of the volute being a design very common in the gold work of the last Minoan period (Evans, *Prehistoric Tombs*, p. 130, Fig. 119, No. 75a). The whole design is highly conventionalized and shows that wherever these vases were made the Palace style was already at an advanced stage of its development.

That these vases also represent a style foreign to the small Minoan towns on the Isthmus of Hierapetra is quite clear, as the clay, technique and whole appearance of the vessels are utterly different from those of the local fabrics. The Zakro filler (*J. H. S.,* XXII, p. 333, and Plate XII), the set of fillers from Palaiokastro (*B. S. A.,* Vol. IX, p. 311, Figs. 9 and 10), all belong to this class; similar also though of slightly earlier date is the fine octopus "*bügelkanne,*" from Gournia (*Gournia,* Pl. H). At Melos also fragments of vases of this class came to light, and these were also regarded as imported fabrics probably from Crete (*Phylakopi,* p. 265, and Plate XXXI, Nos. 1, 2, 3 and 5).

In regard to these fillers which certainly served in religious ceremonies, it is a curious fact that they very seldom occur singly, but always in hoards. In this room were parts of five, a cover decorated with double axes, the basket-shaped vase of Fig. 12 and one of the clay bulls, Pl. IX. At Gournia a number of fillers were found with a bull's head in clay and several vases of curious shape in a small house on the east slope. At Palaiokastro the same

Fig. 12.

thing occurred, so that we may perhaps conclude that each small town possessed a supply of these vessels, which were the property of the village priest and kept in his house.

The basket-shaped vase of Fig. 12 may not be as late as it looks, owing to the character of the design, which does not admit of much freedom of treatment. The curious shape and the abundant use of the double axe show that this vase was probably intended for ritual use.

Another vase closely related to this group from G. 7, R. 1, was found in I. 3, R. 1. It is a very good example of the use made of marine designs, the nautilus, seaweed and rockwork adapting themselves extremely well to vase decoration. The shape of this vase again betrays a metal prototype as shown by the handle where the metal rivet fastening it to the body of the vase has been reproduced in clay.

In J. 12, R. 1, there were found, as stated above, parts of a large plaster relief, evidently that of a woman, if we may judge by her richly embroidered dress and the conventional white color of the skin. The restoration shown in Pl. V combines most of the remaining parts and, except for the left arm, may be considered correct. This left arm may have belonged to another figure, although the other fragments show no signs of the existence of a second relief. The plaster was in so rotten a state that the greater part of the surface had disintegrated beyond hope of recovery; but enough remains to give a vivid idea of the rich character of the dress. The colors are blue, white

Fig. 13.

and yellow, the first two predominating. The work is very delicate and the smallest details are drawn with a care that even now must excite admiration. As is often the case in these Minoan reliefs, the skirt and bust are the parts in highest relief, while the head was not in relief at all, but painted on the flat surface, no fragment of which remains. As in the pottery, we find in Minoan embroidery many of the designs employed in architectural decoration. The border of rosettes on the left sleeve is a design of this sort which

Fig. 14.

also occurs in the jewelry of the later periods (Evans, *Prehistoric Tombs,* p. 130, Fig. 119, No. 66a).

Unfortunately, the work on the bodice has almost disappeared, but enough is left to show that the form was of the usual décolleté type affected by Minoan ladies, which left the breasts exposed. Around her neck are two necklaces. The upper one, from its yellow color, must have been of large gold beads, with festoons of smaller beads hanging from a string of crescent shaped gold bars. The second necklace, which hangs much lower on the bosom, is blue, and no doubt is intended to represent a string of blue porcelain beads, which are often found in Minoan graves of all periods. These reliefs, in gesso duro, have always been found at Knossos associated with the remains of the later Palace, and have been classed as belonging to the Late Minoan II period. Neither at Gournia nor at Palaiokastro were there any traces of such reliefs, and even the rulers of Phaistos and Hagia Triada seem to have contented themselves with fresco painting on a flat surface. That such a thing should have come to light in the ruins of a small town on a barren island is a matter of no small astonishment, and strengthens the idea that this must have been a settlement in close connection with the center of Minoan civilization.

THE STONE VASES.

The fragmentary condition of the pottery on this site was more than made up for by the enormous numbers of stone vases and lamps from all parts of the town. In all they amounted to about eighty-five objects. Hitherto thirty or even twenty stone vases in good condition had been considered a fair output for one season, but here, for some reason, the plunderers left the entire accumulation behind them, with the result that Pseira, from the town and cemetery combined, produced the huge total of 150 stone vases and lamps, of which the majority were in an excellent state of preservation.

Any classification of these vases into distinctive periods is impossible, for, excepting the stone lamps and cup, we find that almost every type of vase found in the Late Minoan I houses has its origin as far back as the Middle Minoan I, or even an earlier period.

The fact of their durability and the labor required to make even a small vase makes it probable that they were in most cases handed down from one generation to another, and the occurrence of a stone vessel in a Late Minoan I deposit gives not the slightest clue as to the date of its manufacture. We know that Pseira, as a town, underwent complete destruction in the Middle Minoan I era, and was not occupied again until the Middle Minoan III period. Therefore, unless the returning settlers brought many stone vases with them, we might assign those found in the Late Minoan I houses to that date. But that these people arrived empty handed, with no goods or chattels, is highly improbable, so that it is best to describe the objects without assigning them to any definite period except in the case of the larger lamps and the stone goblet. Of these lamps three are of the pedestal type, Fig. 15 *d*, and four others with equally large basins stand on only a short foot. All these are

Fig. 15.

of steatite and each has cuttings for two wicks. In addition to these, which are all in a fair state of preservation, a number of pedestals were found from which the lamp basin had been broken away. Several of the lamps on a short foot had the base roughly trimmed, and it seems probable that they were all originally of the pedestal type, but, having been broken off, still continued to be used, the broken base being thrown away as valueless.

Of the small lamps nine are of black steatite, three in reddish limestone and two in pale green steatite of fine quality. One of the red stone lamps, from House B, is shown in Fig. 17, and is a fine example of its class. The collar of drooping leaves is a design which is characteristic of Late Minoan II art.

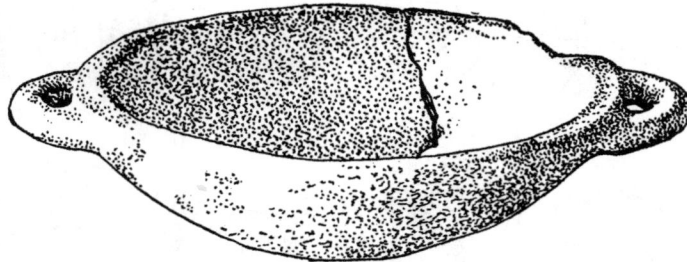

Fig. 16.

Fig. 15 gives the main types of small lamps and vases from the site. Although I know of no pedestal lamps earlier than the Middle Minoan I period, the short type of large lamp certainly occurs earlier, for in the Middle Minoan I House A at Vasiliki, five of this kind were found in 1906, but so rotted that it was impossible to preserve them. Of the smaller lamps, Fig. 15 d certainly belongs to the Late Minoan I period, as the collar of leaves never occurs before that date. The vase c, in the same figure, belongs to a class of vessels which were found in the Koumasa tombs in great numbers and should be assigned to at least the Early Minoan II period. Of the "blossom" bowls, two types, j and k, were found; of these, j is probably the earlier, although k occurs as far back as the Middle Minoan I era. With the type of k the period is indicated by the profile, for the earliest examples have a curving outline, while in those of the Late Minoan I class the shoulder is higher and the outline more angular. The type i is common in the deposits of all periods from the Middle Minoan I to the Late Minoan I period. The large bowl, Fig. 16, is a typical Middle Minoan shape and comes from a house of that date. I do not know of its ever occurring in Late Minoan I deposits, although in the Middle Minoan I houses it is the type most commonly found.

The vase shown in Fig. 15 m, from the road outside House A, closely resembles in shape the famous warrior cup from Hagia Triada. A hammer head in gray veined marble is a type already known by examples from Palaiokastro (B. S. A., Vol. XI, p. 279), and from Hagia Triada (Mon. Ant., XIV, p. 56, Fig. 26). These hammer heads could not have been intended for actual use as such, owing to the fine quality of the stone and the fact that they so seldom show signs of wear.

In Fig. 15 h and l are shown two large steatite vessels, the first from the road by House A, the other from House B, R. 9; of these the second resembles a cooking pot of the present day, while the other is a shape which recalls the much earlier painted pots so common in the Early Minoan III epoch, although it is not likely to be of that date, owing to the fine quality of the

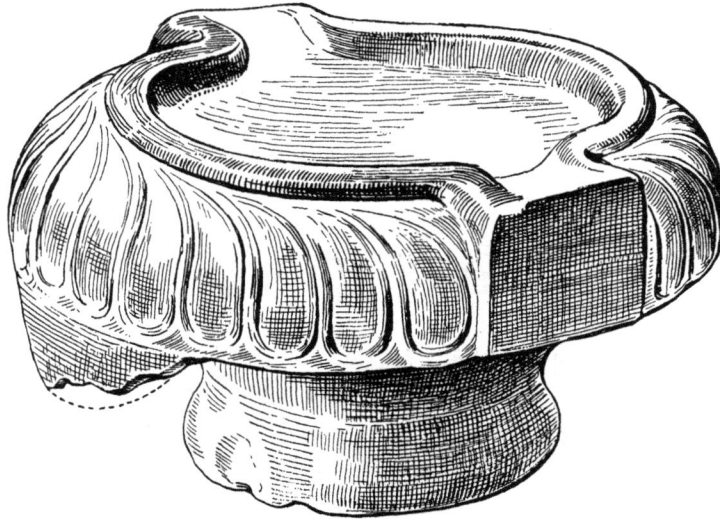

Fig. 17.

steatite. The black steatite in use in the earlier period is, as a rule, very poor in quality and quite inferior to that used for the better class of Late Minoan I stone vases.

The best of the stone vases found at Pseira is the splendid vessel shown in Plate VIII, which exactly duplicates one found at Knossos (*B. S. A.,* Vol. VI, 1899-1900, p. 30). The stone is a species of breccia of very hard quality, which occurs in large masses close to the site, possibly indicating that the vase

Fig. 18.

was made in the town. The house in which it was found, D. 5, R. 1, on the south hill, was characteristic of the Late Minoan I era, which would place this vase in that period, while those of Knossos were assigned to the Late Minoan II period. Just below the carved rim the vase is pierced on each side by two small holes, which were probably used for suspending it by means of cords when it was not in use.

In the big house B parts of three delicate cups of white marble were found of the type of Pl. X *d,* and also two fragments of a marble plaque on which can be seen rows of ashlar masonry, evidently the walls of a large building. From the curiously irregular shape of this plaque, of which no two sides are of the same length, we conclude that it must have been part of a mosaic representing some sort of scene with buildings in the background.

The only remaining object which presents any new features is the pretty lamp of Fig. 19, which comes from House B, Rooms 4, 5 and 7. It is of the finest quality of brownish steatite and repeats the idea of the "blossom" bowls, only here the flower is open instead of partly closed, as is usually the case. The workmanship is excellent, the carving in very sharp relief, and,

Fig. 19.

with the exception of the vase in Pl. VIII, this lamp is the best example of Minoan stone cutting found on the site. Although the vases were very numerous, it will be seen that they were confined to the very limited number of types shown in Fig. 15, which were picked out as the best examples of each variety.

Two knife pommels in marble and a gold riveted blade show that the weapons were on a par with the other possessions of these Minoan villagers, but the scarcity of bronze in comparison with Gournia indicates that the sack of Pseira was of a more thorough nature than was the case with its mainland neighbor.   RICHARD B. SEAGER.

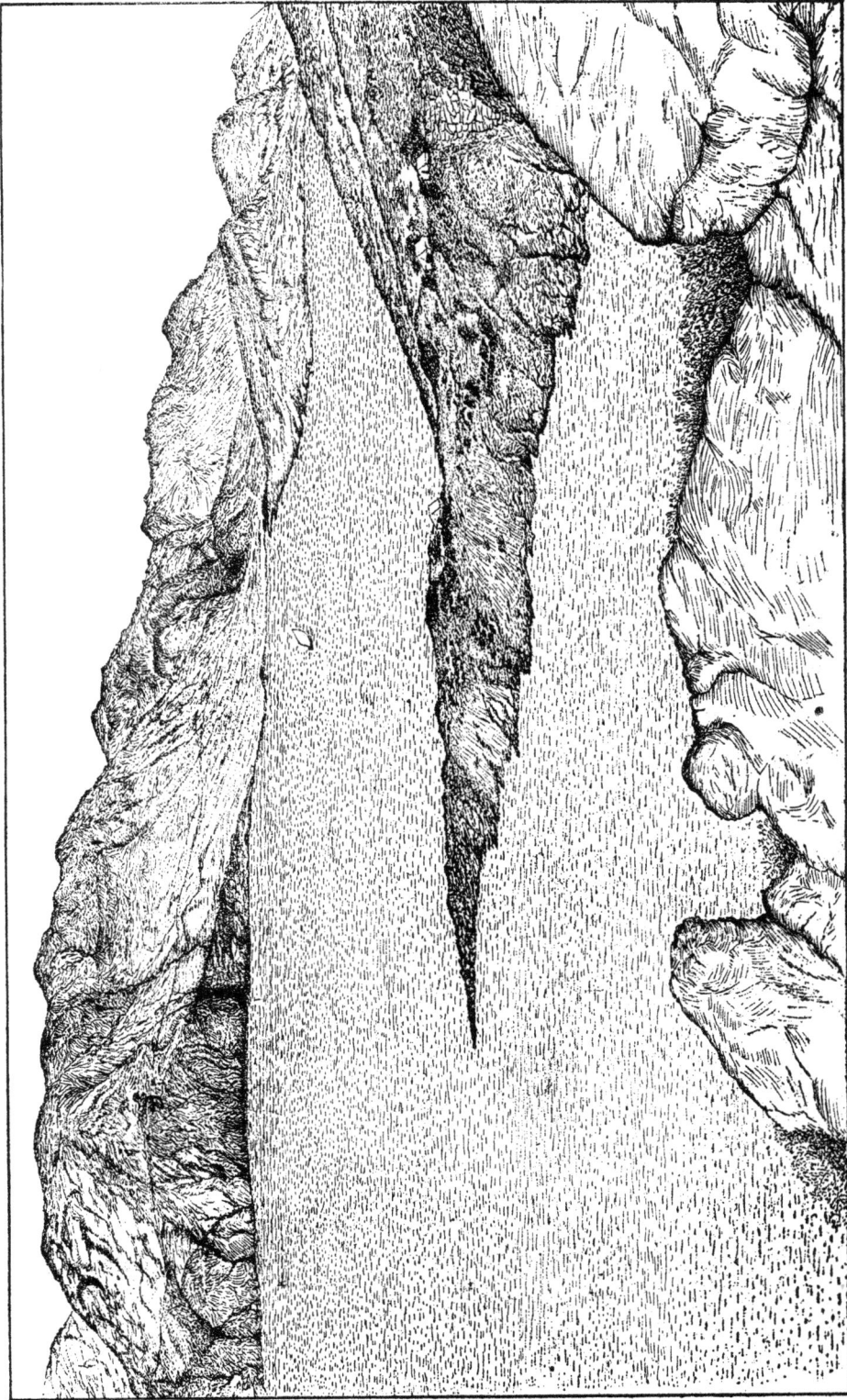

Sketch Showing Coves and Site of Pseira with the Coast of Crete in the Background.

PLATE III

VIEW OF THE TOWN OF PSEIRA SHOWING EXCAVATIONS OF 1907

COCKAYNE—BOSTON

PLATE IV

PSEIRA. THE LANDING PLACE FROM THE COVE AND THE STAIRWAY LEADING TO THE TOWN

COCKAYNE—BOSTON

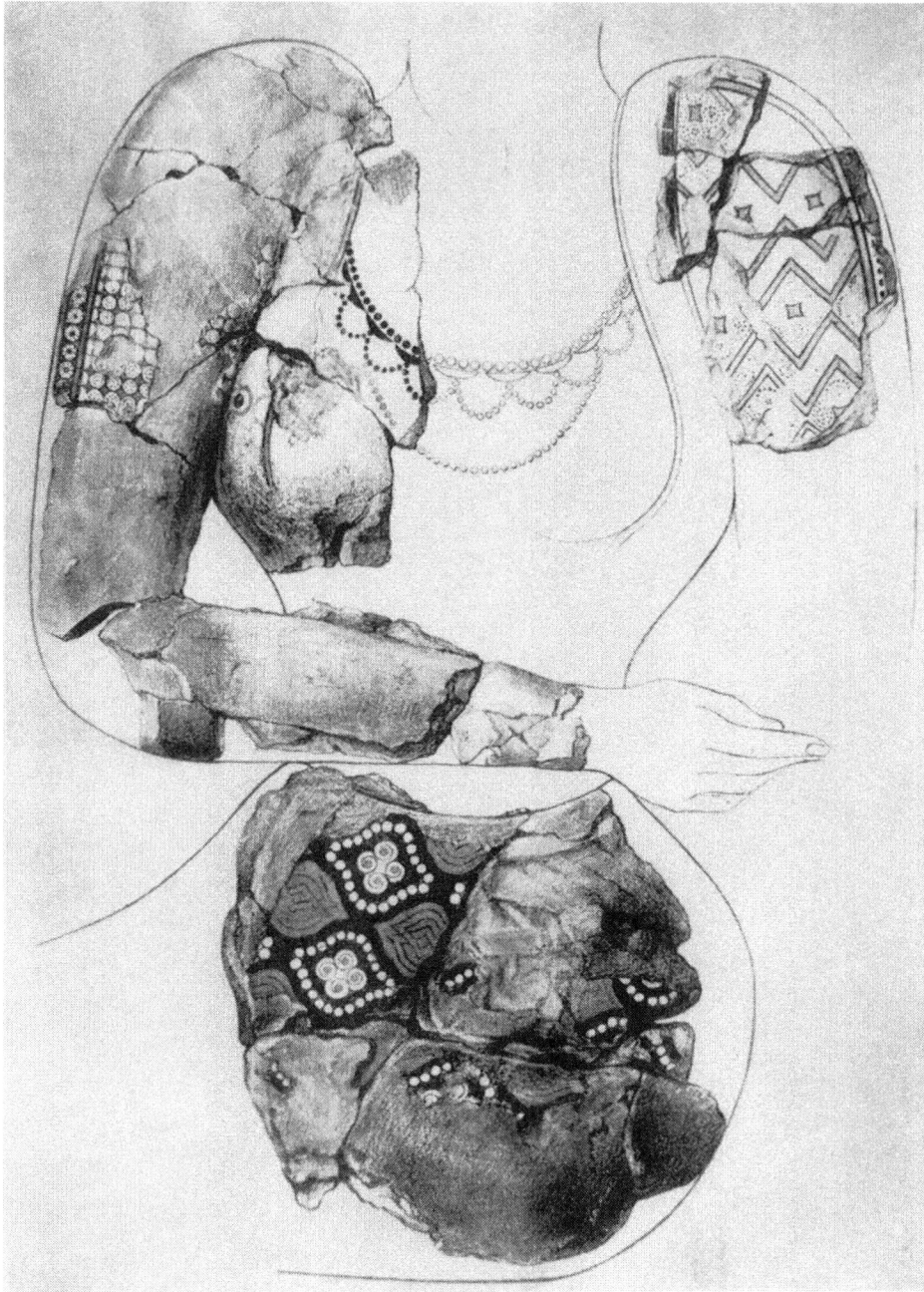

PSEIRA. FRAGMENTS OF A PAINTED RELIEF WITH OUTLINES PARTLY RESTORED

PSEIRA. A AND B MIDDLE MINOAN I CUPS. C LATE MINOAN I JUG

PSEIRA LATE MINOAN I VASE

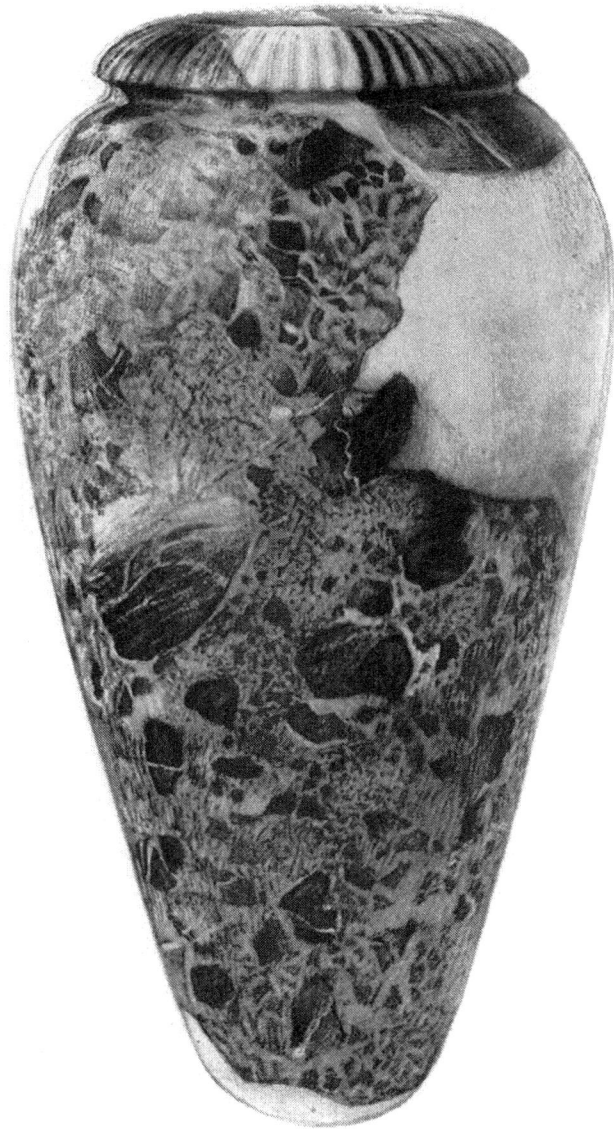

PSEIRA BRECCIA VASE

PLATE IX

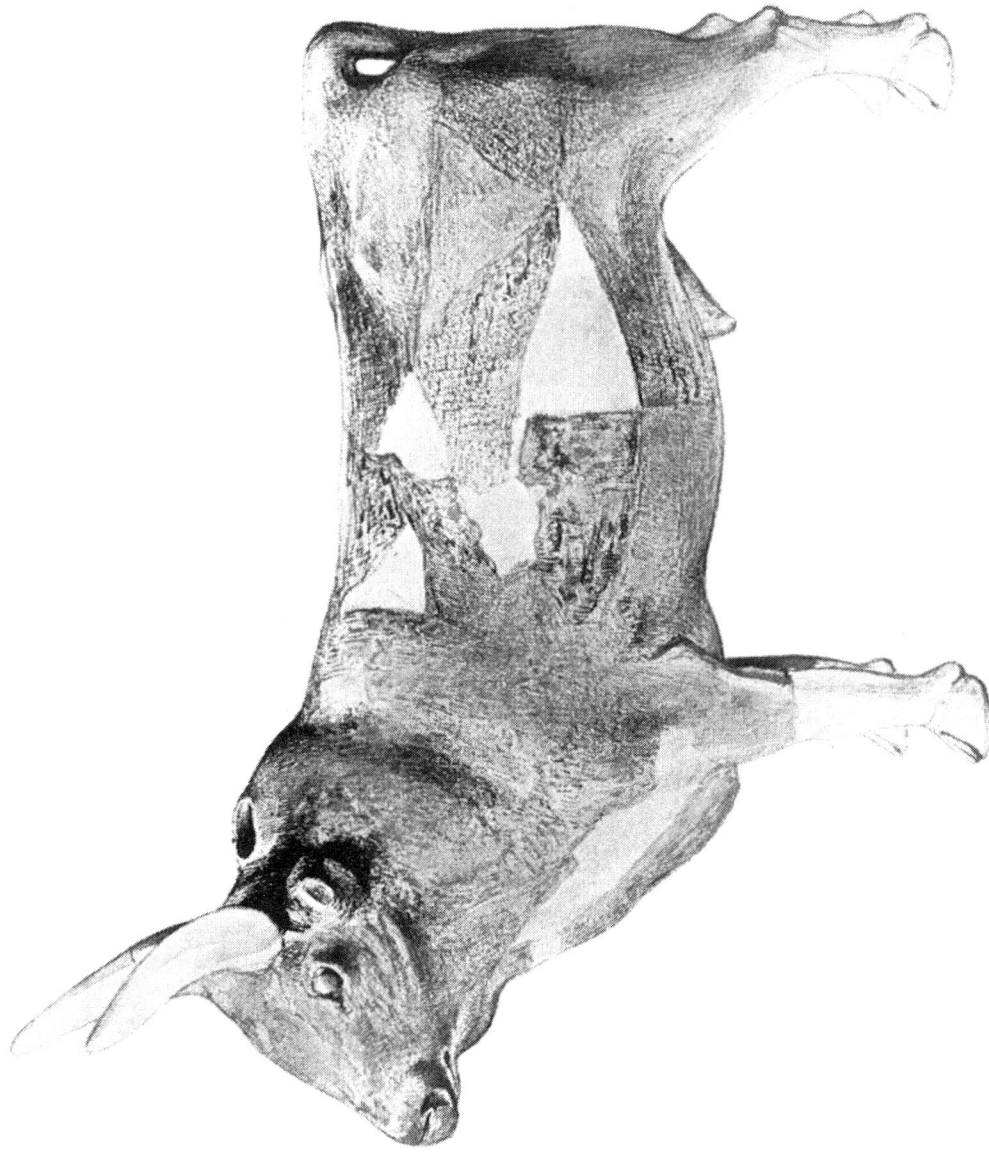

PSEIRA TERRA COTTA BULL

UNIVERSITY OF PENNSYLVANIA

THE UNIVERSITY MUSEUM

ANTHROPOLOGICAL PUBLICATIONS

VOL. VII   No. 1

THE CEMETERY OF PACHYAMMOS, CRETE

BY

RICHARD B. SEAGER

PHILADELPHIA

PUBLISHED BY THE UNIVERSITY MUSEUM

1916

ABBREVIATIONS

The following abbreviations have been employed in the text.

A.J.A.	American Journal of Archæology.
B.S.A.	Annual of the British School at Athens.
Gournia	Gournia, The American Exploration Society, Philadelphia, 1909.
Isopata	The Prehistoric Tombs of Knossos, by A. J. Evans.
Mochlos	Explorations on the Island of Mochlos, American School of Classical Studies, 1912, by R. B. Seager.
Phylakopi	Phylakopi, Society for the Promotion of Hellenic Studies, London, 1904.
Pseira	Excavations on the Island of Pseira, Crete, Anthropological Publications, The Museum, University of Pennsylvania, Vol. III, No. 1.
Sphoungaras	Excavations in Eastern Crete, Sphoungaras, Anthropological Publications, The Museum, University of Pennsylvania, Vol. III, No. 2.
Vasiliki	Excavations at Vasiliki, 1904 and 1906, Transactions, Department of Archæology, University of Pennsylvania, Vol. I, Part III, 1905, and Vol. II, Part II, 1907.
E.M.I.	Early Minoan I.
E.M.II.	Early Minoan II.
E.M.III.	Early Minoan III.
M.M.I.	Middle Minoan I.
M.M.II.	Middle Minoan II.
M M.III.	Middle Minoan III.
L.M.I.	Late Minoan I.
L.M.II.	Late Minoan II.
L.M.III.	Late Minoan III.

THE CEMETERY OF PACHYAMMOS, CRETE

In Eastern Crete at the head of the gulf of Mirabello lies the Isthmus of Hierapetra. The mountain chains of the Lasithi group and the Triptite range, further to the east, are sharply divided at this point by an almost level valley which stretches from the northern coast on the gulf of Mirabello across to the plain of Hierapetra facing the southern or Libyan sea. The island is only about seven miles wide at this point and this narrow valley must have formed in all periods an important highway between the north and south coasts. To a maritime people this must have been especially useful as the voyage by sea to and from Hierapetra around the eastern end of the island with its far-flung rocky capes was, at best, a hazardous one in this land of sudden gales where places of shelter for shipping are so few and far between.

The Isthmus offered an easy means of avoiding this circuit as merchandise could be carried across from north to south or vice versa and re-shipped to its final destination.

The Hierapetra plain is the most fertile portion of Eastern Crete and, as it lies at the point of the island nearest to Egypt, must have had a considerable amount of trade with the latter. The Greek coinage of Hierapetra and the numerous remains still extant of the Roman city show its importance in the classical period when it ranked as the chief town of this part of the island.

It seems clear from our knowledge of the Minoan civilization that, in certain stages of its development, it was in close touch with Egypt. From Egyptian art it borrowed much and, in turn, gave much. We find both Cretan objects on Egyptian sites and vice versa. It is therefore not unlikely that, in Minoan times, this trade route across the Isthmus played its part in the communication between the two countries which would account for the numerous Minoan settlements that are constantly coming to light at the head of the gulf of Mirabello.

In 1902–1904 Mrs. Hawes and her expedition excavated the prosperous and well-preserved town site of Gournia on the coast and another site, Vasiliki, which lies a mile or so inland on the Isthmus.

In 1907 Pseira, a settlement on a small rocky island lying in the gulf opposite the Isthmus, was cleared and since then evidence has accumulated which shows that villages of more or less importance existed in the Kavusi valley, at Vraïka, Monasteraki and Pachyammos with which last this report is chiefly concerned.

These sites, Gournia, Pachyammos, Vasiliki, Monasteraki, Vraïka and Kavusi all lie within a radius of three miles on the northern end of the Isthmus while Pseira, the island site, is also close at hand. The land along this part of the coast is not particularly fertile and suffers greatly from winter storms which drive the salt spray far inland thus blighting the crops. Today only three of these sites are inhabited villages, Kavusi, Vasiliki and Monasteraki. The first two contain roughly 800 and 400 people respectively. Monasteraki can boast of only a dozen families. Pachyammos is the modern port and when I saw it first in 1903 it consisted of a few warehouses and a couple of roadside inns though it now contains ten dwelling houses.

It is clear therefore that the present day population of this district is less than in Minoan times and the fertility of the soil does not seem to warrant a larger one. We must infer that its ancient importance was principally due to a road crossing the island at this point more useful in the days of small sailing craft than in our era of steamships.

There is no real harbor at the northern end of the Isthmus. The Tholos of Kavusi and Gournia are both open roadsteads. The rocky point at Pachyammos offers a partial shelter for small craft in all but the worst storms. In Minoan times, before the subsidence of the coast so noticeable in this part of the island, the shelter may have been better as the reef of rock stretching out from the end of the point may have then broken the force of the waves whereas today it is almost completely submerged. At any rate, Pachyammos, poor harbor as it is, must have been the principal northern port of the Isthmus and it has always seemed odd that there were such scanty traces of a Minoan settlement at this point.

The shore at Gournia, which lies about twenty minutes walk to the west of Pachyammos over two hilly ridges, could offer no shelter of any sort for shipping. In Minoan times Gournia was the principal town of the district and, for lack of anything better, seemed to have been the starting point of our supposed trade route across the Isthmus.

Owing to recent discoveries we can now correct this error and Pachyammos assumes its natural position as a place of importance in ancient times and the site of a Minoan port.

In October, 1913, the northern villages of the Isthmus suffered severely from one of the torrential rains which sometimes visit the island of Crete. In such a bare mountainous land these storms can work a vast amount of damage in a very short space of time. Owing to the lack of vegetation on the mountain sides, there is nothing to check the torrents of water which, in their struggle to reach the sea, tear great channels through the terraced fields and the level land along the coast. A similar storm at Zakro in Crete is graphically described by Mr. Hogarth in his "Accidents of an Antiquarian's Life."

In the storm of 1913 the hamlet of Pachyammos suffered severely. The water rose to the height of a metre in the low-lying houses and only by tearing down a long piece of wall between the two village inns were the houses saved from destruction. The mass of water thus released tore its way to the sea some 150 metres distant leaving a broad channel twenty metres in width and a metre in depth to mark its course. When the water finally subsided it was seen that part of a Minoan cemetery of jar-burials had been brought to light in this channel. Some twelve jars were standing along the edge of the eastern bank formed by the torrent while fragments of others strewing the ground showed that a certain number had been broken up by the rush of water.

As soon as the weather permitted, excavations were begun which lasted from April 8 to May 9, 1914. On my return to Crete work was resumed for a fortnight in January, 1915, in order to make sure that the limits of the cemetery had been reached and that no more jars remained in the vicinity.

This burial ground lies in the broad sand beach which gives Pachyammos (Deep Sand) its name. The space occupied by the cemetery was roughly a parallelogram, 150 metres long by 40 metres wide, and lying some 20 metres back from the sea.

The cemetery furnished additional proof to that already gained at Pseira (Pseira, p. 16) and Mochlos of the subsidence of this part of the Cretan coast. Fully half the burial jars were found standing in sea-water and it seems hardly probable that this was the case at the time of interment. Every one knows the difficulty of digging a pit in wet sand and it is not likely that the Minoans undertook the difficult task of placing their jars in holes which filled with sea-water when ten metres further back from the sea they would have had a dry sandy soil in which to place their dead.

The cemetery seems to have continued in use from very early times down to the L. M. I period. The discovery of child burials in E. M. III pots, a small oval larnax of apparently the same date and a few stone vases of the early type sufficed to show that the first burials were contemporary with those discovered at Mochlos, Pseira and the Gournia cemetery at Sphoungaras. (Seager, Mochlos, and Hall, Sphoungaras.) Whereas at Mochlos and Pseira the greater number of graves dated from the E. M. period, here the M. M. I, M. M. III and early L. M. I periods play the most important part in the history of the cemetery. The Sphoungaras burials also dated chiefly from these same periods and there one was struck by the paucity of small objects placed with the dead in contrast with the profusion of jewelry, weapons and vases that accompany Early Minoan interments. (Sphoungaras, p. 66.) In point of small objects the Pachyammos cemetery was even less productive and the majority of burial jars contained nothing but fragmentary human remains. In a few cases some clay cups and small vases were found in the jars, but this was the exception rather than the rule. Unlike Sphoungaras no seal-stones occurred with any of the interments and yet, judging by the quality of the burial jars themselves, one would have supposed the people buried at Pachyammos to have been superior in point of worldly wealth to those buried at Sphoungaras.

The Pachyammos cemetery produced in all 213 burial jars and six larnakes, whereas at Sphoungaras only 150 jars and one larnax were found, but the latter site had suffered more from the action of time and denudation of the soil than was the case at Pachyammos.

There seemed to have been no rule as to the depth at which the jars were placed. Some were found within 20 centimetres of the surface, others at a depth of 2.50 metres which would lead one to suppose that the question of depth depended solely on the energy or wishes of the families of the deceased.

The digging in the soft beach sand was extremely easy until the water level was reached. Below this level work was very difficult as constant bailing was necessary and the falling in of the soft sand banks delayed progress. In many places below the water level the sand around the jars, through some chemical action, had hardened into a stony formation and it required much care and patience on the part of the workmen to extract the jar from its hard bed without breakage. The clay of the jars, after so many centuries of dampness, was very friable and it is remarkable that any of them hung together. Strangely enough, in most cases, painted designs were remarkably well preserved in spite of the wet and offered, in this respect, a great contrast to the dry hillside cemeteries of Mochlos, Pseira and Sphoungaras where the painted surfaces of the jars and vases were usually much destroyed.

The cemetery of Pachyammos came as a complete surprise as there are no traces of an extensive town site in the neighborhood. The soil of the hill of Alatzo Mouri, which rises above the warehouses of the little port, is filled with Minoan potsherds but there are no signs of house walls. This hillside has been much denuded and it is possible that the stones from the early houses may have been used for modern field walls though there are not enough of these to account for the disappearance of the entire house walls of a fairly large village. The only other possible site for the town would be in the valley lying back from the sea behind the cemetery. Here the soil is deep and there would naturally be few remains on the surface. Local tradition points to this spot and various peasants have told me that their fathers and grandfathers had turned up vases and weapons in these fields in former years.

One of the most noticeable features of the cemetery is the evidence of the utter disregard of the Minoans for the graves of their forebears. It was a common occurrence to find a group of burial jars broken and tumbled about in the greatest confusion and upright in the midst of the wreckage an unbroken jar, the placing of which was responsible for the destruction of the earlier interments. The Pachyammos cemetery did not offer such good evidence as that of Sphoungaras for the method of placing the bodies in the jars. At Pachyammos the skeletal remains were of the most fragmentary nature, but what little evidence could be gathered tended to show that, as at Sphoungaras (Sphoungaras, p. 61) the body was placed in a sitting posture, the knees trussed up under the chin and the arms doubled back against the body.

The burials were primary burials, that is to say, the body had been placed in the jar shortly after death. In the case of secondary interments the body is first allowed to decay and when the flesh has quite disappeared the dry bones are collected and given a final burial.

The skeletal remains at Sphoungaras showed clearly that the bodies were placed in the jars with the head downward. The jar was then placed in the ground bottom up so that the corpse occupied a sitting or rather a crouching position.

Very few skulls could be saved and from the entire cemetery there are only four examples.

In these cemeteries one is constantly struck by the small size of the jars used for interments and in many cases it is difficult to understand how they could have contained an adult body although we know that the Minoans were a small boned race with a low average stature. Of course many of the smaller jars probably contained the bodies of children but the proportion of small jars is very great and in only one case was a jar found capable of containing a body of a really large person. In a few cases a jar with a narrow neck had had the rim carefully chipped away to allow more room for the insertion of the corpse but this was the exception rather than the rule. I think it will probably be found that, in many cases, the hip bones and the collar bones were intentionally broken in order to insert bodies into jars of the type shown in Pl. XVI, No. XII, C, whereas with jars like those of Pl. II, No. II, a, this would not have been necessary as we proved by experiments on our workmen at Sphoungaras. (Sphoungaras, p. 61.)

Mrs. Dohan (Miss Hall) suggests (Sphoungaras, p. 62) that the bodies were probably trussed up immediately after death or perhaps even before death had actually taken place.

At Pachyammos in no instance were the jars found bedded on a layer of beach pebbles as was so often the case at Sphoungaras. (Sphoungaras, p. 59.) In many cases pithoi were found neatly built around with large stones to hold them more securely in position.

The jars often occurred in groups of from three to five or more which would lead one to suppose that each group might represent the various members of a single family. This may have been the case in some instances but often the jars of a group belonged to widely different periods so that it would be unsafe to attach much importance to this grouping which must sometimes have been accidental.

As far as could be seen there was nothing above the jars in the surface soil to mark their position and if any such mark ever had existed it was probably of wood or other perishable material. It was either owing to the absence of any mark at all or to its perishable nature that the later interments caused such havoc among the earlier burials. As I have said before, the Minoan gravedigger was no respecter of rights and once his pit was begun he carried it down to the desired depth irrespective of the fact that he had happened to start his work directly over ground already occupied by earlier burials. In one case an intrusive child burial had been placed in a jar already containing an older interment. The bottom of the jar had been broken in and, without removing it from the soil, the child's corpse was shoved in at the broken end which was then covered by a large fragment of broken pottery.

The small oval tubs or larnakes which had tightly fitting covers were placed in the ground in an upright position but oddly enough the large oval and square larnakes, equally possessed of covers, were put in upside down. As at Sphoungaras (Sphoungaras, p. 60), it was clear that the Minoans did not always give their best jars for the burial of their dead and if the household happened to possess a damaged specimen it was considered quite good enough for a coffin. Thus one found jars lacking parts of the rim, handles missing and in several cases the bottom half of a previously broken pithos was used to cover a child's body.

There are some ten or twelve different types of pithoi represented in the cemetery but all of them are commonly to be found as store jars in Minoan house ruins with the exception of those noted at Sphoungaras (Sphoungaras, Fig. 36), and shown here in Pl. II, No. II, a. This type, to my knowledge, has not been found on any of the town sites in this neighborhood and was probably intended solely for burial purposes for which its shape is peculiarly suited.

The decoration of the painted jars varied according to their date but one type of decoration, if it can be so called, ran through all the periods represented in the cemetery. This is the drip pattern, Plates V and XVI, always a great favorite in the history of Minoan ceramics. It occurred on 78 of the 213 pithoi found in the cemetery. They were associated with burial groups of all dates from the Early Minoan to the Late Minoan periods. This style was noted at Vasiliki in Early Minoan context (Excavations at Vasiliki, 1904, p. 11) and has perhaps the right to claim the longest life of any type of Minoan decorative design as no other can be traced through so many successive periods.

It is difficult to assign burial jars from a cemetery of this sort to their proper periods. It is almost impossible to say whether an unpainted pithos, neither containing nor associated with any small objects, is of Early, Middle, or Late Minoan date. So far no careful attempt has been made to classify pithoi according to their shape alone and until this has been done one has no criterion by which to judge them. Of these unpainted pithoi the only type which it seemed possible to date, both at Sphoungaras and Pachyammos, is that shown in Pl. III which appears to belong definitely to the M. M. III and L. M. I periods and to represent the closing stage in the history of these two cemeteries. It is this type that is so often responsible for the havoc wrought among the Early and Middle

Minoan burials and for that reason was always regarded with considerable disfavor during the excavation of the cemetery.

The dating of the painted jars is much easier as in most cases both the paint and style of decoration enable one to assign them to their proper place in the chronological sequence of Minoan ceramics with a fair degree of certainty. The most difficult question is to distinguish between the jars of the M. M. III and L. M. I periods as here the dividing line is not clearly defined. I think it would be advisable to recast these two periods using as a line of demarcation between them the marked decrease in the use of white paint as a superadded color for picking out the details of a dark design on a light ground. The use of the Late Minoan red paint is another good means of distinguishing L. M. I from M. M. III vases as this red is of a very different quality from that used in the Middle Minoan period.

I have not attempted to give a description of all the pithoi found in the cemetery. The majority of them are without any especial interest so that in the following account I have mentioned only those which, either by their decoration, shape or context, deserve notice.

As far as possible I have dealt with the jars according to the groups in which they were found. In the following catalogue these groups are represented by Roman numerals and the individual jars of each group are lettered, *i. e.* No. XI, b, is jar b of group XI. For the sake of convenience in cases where a jar was found alone, not associated with a definite group, I have given it a Roman numeral to itself.

I. The first group of interest contained the M. M. I jar shown in Pl. I, No. I, a. It was found to overlie the small E. M. III pot, No. I, b, of Pl. II, which contained the well preserved skeleton of a small infant and a cup of coarse clay. Near at hand, on a level with the M. M. I jar, lay the oval larnax of Pl. III and a small M. M. I pithos similar to those shown in Pl. XI. The larnax has a very primitive look. It is made of coarse clay and bears traces of a design which definitely dates it as belonging to the M. M. I period. This design is identical with that shown on the M. M. I jars in Pl. XI and is applied in dark paint on the light ground of the clay. A larnax of similar shape was found some years ago at Stavroménos near Candia in a M. M. I grave and thus far larnakes of this oval type have not been found in either M. M. III or L. M. I deposits. The two M. M. I jars of this group are examples of a style of decoration characteristic of the period. (Pseira, p. 19, Fig. 4.) (Sphoungaras p. 60, Fig. 32.) Near this group stood the fine M. M. III jar of Plates I and IV, No. I, d. It is a good example of the final stages of the light on dark style and the design of shell spirals shows strongly the influence of the succeeding L. M. I period. (See L. M. I jar from Mochlos, A. J. A., Vol. XIII, 1909, Pl. XI.) The marbled pattern of white paint on the base is occasionally met with in the Middle Minoan period both in the dark on light and light on dark wares. This pattern is evidently meant to imitate the breccia used for stone vases. (Pseira, Pl. VIII.) The wreath on the shoulder is very characteristic of the later Palace Style pottery of the L. M. II period. (Isopata, Pl. C, 1.) There are scallops of white paint around the base, the neck and the rim and wavy white lines on the upper part of the latter. M. M. III jars of similar type were found at Sphoungaras. (Sphoungaras, p. 62, Fig. 34, and p. 63, Fig. 35.)

II. The next group contained two broken unpainted pithoi of the type shown in Pl. II, No. II, a, and several small pithoi covered with drip pattern of the type of those shown in Pl. V, Nos. 1, 3, 5. Three of these jars contained unpainted L. M. I cups of the ordinary handleless type. (Gournia, Pl. II, No. 13.)

III. The jar of Plates I and VI, No. III, was found standing by itself. The design is a curious one and probably belongs to the border line between the M. M. III and L. M. I periods as it shares the characteristics of both the light on dark and dark on light styles of these two periods. The cross-shaped masses of dark paint on the broad buff band about the middle of the jar evidently represent a fully opened blossom. The centers of these blossoms are picked out by circles of white paint and white lines and dots outline the edges of the petals. On the dark paint of the shoulder is a narrow band of white spirals passing just under the handles. There may have been another similar band higher up but the painted surface of this portion of the jar is very badly preserved. There are thin white lines around the base which is covered with dark paint.

IV. The next group contained five jars all buried at a considerable depth. Three of these bear the drip pattern, one is unpainted, type of Pl. II, No. II, a, and the fifth is the jar of Pl. I, No. IV, a, which dates from early in the L. M. I period. The design of marguerites is frequently met with in this period. (Gournia, Pl. VIII, No. 21.) (Sphoungaras, p. 67, Fig. 39.) Like the jar Pl. I, No. III the blossoms show signs of having been picked out in white and there was a similar band of white spirals on the shoulder. The body of this jar is covered with a thin coat of marbled brown paint. In the surface soil over this group stood the small pithos of Pl. XVI, No. IV, b, which is chiefly noticeable for the spout at the base, an additional proof that many of these jars were primarily intended for household use.

V. A small drip pattern pithos contained two cups, one of a low open type covered with mottled red paint and a small grey and white marble bowl. (See Mochlos, Pl. IX, No. III, a.) One can not date this pithos with any certainty but the stone bowl would appear to belong to either the E. M. III or M. M. I periods.

VI. This group contained an amphora of coarse clay and five pithoi, only one of which was unbroken. With the exception of a M. M. I jar, of the type of Pl. XI, they were all unpainted. With this group were found two cups of which one, covered with black paint with a band of white spirals around the rim, is shown in Pl. II, No. VI, a. Similar cups are common on all the sites in this neighborhood. (Gournia, Pl. C, No. 4.) This type which first appears late in the M. M. III period runs on into the L. M. I age.

VII. There were three jars in this group, two of which were covered with drip pattern. The third is the large unpainted pot shown in Pl. VII, No. VII. One of the drip pithoi contained a small breccia bowl. (Type of Mochlos, Pl. IX, No. III, a.) Near the other pithos and the large pot lay two steatite bowls.

These stone vases may be the remains of an Early Minoan interment. They are probably earlier in date than the jars with which they were found as the large pot, judging by the clay, would seem to belong to the L. M. I period. The two drip pithoi may be older.

VIII. Of the eight pithoi which formed this group only two are worthy of notice. One of them contained three unpainted cups of Middle Minoan date. (See Gournia, Pl. VI,

No. 3.) The other jar is that shown in Pl. VIII, No. VIII. It is not easy to date this jar exactly as it might belong to either the M. M. I or M. M. III periods. Dark designs edged with white as in this example frequently occur in the M. M. I period. (Pseira, Pl. VI, a and b.) On the other hand the clay and quality of the paint are more like those used for M. M. III pottery. The design is rather meaningless. Between the handles are groups of four circles of dark paint. Under the handles are three vertical curving bands or sprays also in dark paint. These sprays and the circles are picked out in white and there is a badly preserved band of white spirals around the neck. Around the base are dark bands edged with white.

IX. This group, which lay underneath a field wall, was composed of five much broken pithoi of various dates piled one on top of another in the greatest confusion. In the midst of the wreckage stood a sixth pithos of M. M. III or L. M. I date of the type of those shown on the left in Pl. II. This later interment was apparently responsible for the damage caused to the earlier burial jars which were broken up to make room for it. The two earliest jars are of M. M. I date of the type of those shown in Pl. XI. One of them contained two M. M. I cups of which one showed traces of a white paint design on a dark ground. The third jar, a drip pithos, contained an unpainted cup of similar date. The two best jars from this group are those shown in Plates VIII and IX, No. IX, a, and Plate X. Both of them belong to the end of the M. M. III or beginning of the L. M. I period.

The jar of Pl. IX bears a spirited design of dolphins in dark paint edged with white on a buff ground. The design of Pl. X is curious and it is hard to decide whether the artist wished to represent an ankh-like motive or something taken from nature. The design is picked out with white paint and there is a wreath, also in white, around the neck. Both these jars are interesting examples of the period of transition linking the M. M. III and L. M. I periods. That of Pl. IX has a decided artistic merit and may not unfairly be compared with the well known flying fish and dolphin frescoes from Phylakopi (Phylakopi, Pl. III) and Knossos. (B. S. A., Vol. VIII, 1901–02, p. 58.) The latter is shown in Pl. XV.

Near this group lay the unpainted jar of Pl. XII, No. IX, c. Jars of this type often occur in M. M. III deposits and are always unpainted. This example, which was of very poor clay, contained a much corroded child's bangle of bronze. It was a perfectly plain metal hoop of which over half had disappeared owing to the action of sea-water.

X. The larnax of Pl. XII, No. X, a, was the next object to come to light (length 73 cm., width 41 cm., depth 42.05 cm.). It is made of very coarse red clay and had been placed in the soil upside down, its cover lying underneath it. The weight of the sand had long since crushed in the bottom and on clearing the larnax, no objects were found with the exception of a few teeth. This larnax is probably later in date than the oval one of Pl. III. We must nevertheless assign it to some time in the Middle Minoan period on the evidence of similar larnakes found in a M. M. I ossuary at Vasiliki in 1904. (Vasiliki, Trans. Vol. II. Pt. 2, p. 115.)

Near this larnax in the surface soil a drip pattern pithos was found standing in an upright position instead of being placed upside down as was the usual custom. A large fragment of pottery had been used as a cover for the neck. This pithos contained a small jug and a cup. The jug bears a band of spirals in dark paint around the shoulder and a ripple design on the base. The cup which has white spirals on a dark ground resembles those shown in Pl. II, Nos. VI, a, and XIII, b. These two objects, which show both the light on dark and dark on light techniques existing side by side, date from the transitional stage between the M. M. III and L. M. I periods and could equally well belong to either of them.

XI. Near by stood the small jar of Pl. VIII, No. XI, a. It is a remarkably well preserved example of the M. M. III period. The clay is very hard and fine grained which may account for the excellent condition of the painted surface. The decoration consists of two bands of dark paint edged with white around the middle of the jar and these bands are further ornamented by a design of running loops of white paint. There are also dark bands around the rim and base with superadded bands of white.

The fine jar of Pl. XIII, No. XI, b, stood more or less by itself and seemed to belong to no well defined group. This, also, is very well preserved. The design suggests a further development of the octopus motive shown on the fine M. M. II pot found by Mr. Dawkins in the Kamares cave. (B. S. A., Vol. XIX, p. 22, and Pl. X.) Naturalism had made a great advance in the intervening period and was gradually approaching the stage when the L. M. I potters were able to produce such masterpieces of maritime decoration as the octopus jar from Gournia. (Gournia, Pl. H.) The period when vases such as the one from Gournia were produced does not seem to have been of long duration and by the L. M. II period the octopus design is degenerating. The octopus on the L. M. II vase from Isopata (Isopata, Pl. C) has reverted to a type more nearly akin to that on the burial jar which we are describing. By the L. M. III period this design has become still more stylized and debased until it ends in two meaningless waving arms and the complete disappearance of the body of the octopus. This jar, like so many from the cemetery, appears to belong to a transitional stage between the M. M. III and L. M. I periods.

While jars such as those shown in Plates IV, XIV and XXI were still being made the dark on light technique was gradually becoming more and more popular. This octopus jar belongs to this dark on light class and, in point of time, is but slightly, if at all, later than the black and white jars just mentioned. On the other hand, judging by the paint and clay, it is more closely akin to the L. M. I wares than it is to the light on dark M. M. III vases. It, therefore, becomes a question whether we shall divide these periods on the basis of technique or from a chronological point of view. If we go by the former rule, vases like this octopus jar and those of Plates VI, IX, X and XVIII might fall into the L. M. I period, although chronologically they are of the same date as those which we have assigned to the M. M. III age.

To my mind these dark on light vases share the characteristics of both the M. M. III and L. M. I periods to such a marked degree that I have not been willing to throw them bodily into either period, but have contented myself by regarding them as a transitional stage linking the M. M. III wares to those of the L. M. I period.

On this part of the site at a very low level the E. M. III pot of Pl. XI, No. XI, c, came to light. Like many of the smaller pots, it stood upright in the sand. The white design of cross-hatched circles and lozenges filling the triangular spaces between the narrow lines of white is very characteristic of the E. M. III period. The upper half of the pot is covered with black paint, the lower half is plain buff clay.

XII. The next group comprised four jars. Two of them were painted and are shown in Pl. XIII, Nos. XII, a and b, and Pl. XIV. Both belong to the M. M. III period. In No. XII, a, the lower half of the jar is covered with black paint deeply scalloped along the upper edge. The edges of the scallops are picked out with white dots and there are two white bands near the base. Otherwise, save for a narrow dark band on the shoulder and on the rim, the jar is unpainted. The design here reproduced in the medium of clay and paint greatly resembles that found on many carved steatite vases. (Pseira, p. 35, Fig. 15, Nos. j and k.) Stone vases of this type are very common on most Minoan sites and are evidently meant to represent the blossom of a flower, possibly the common anemone.

The other pithos, Pl. XIII, No. XII, b, and Pl. XIV, is entirely covered with black paint on which a marine picture of dolphins, waves and the pebbly sea bottom is worked out in white. The dolphins fill a broad zone around the middle of the jar. Above them is the tossing surface of the sea with clouds of spray blown about by the wind. Below the dolphins is the sea floor dotted with round pebbles. There are white wreath-like designs on the neck and white scallops around the rim. The base is lacking.

This jar is particularly interesting as it shows the preliminary steps by which the highly naturalistic marine designs on L. M. I pottery were attained. In that period we have the finished product. The artist had learnt how much to leave out and how he could adapt his subject to the medium in which he was working. In this early effort the painter attempted too much. The result is that we have rather the effect of an aquarium seen through the glass front, a picture hardly adapted for vase painting. In spite of this the jar has a certain charm, a naïveté, which attracts one with the promise of better things to come.

The fish as a decorative motive certainly dates back to the M. M. I period, to which epoch belongs a series of jugs, painted with white fish, found at Vasiliki. (Vasiliki, Trans., Vol. II, Part 2, Pl. XXX.) In these primitive examples the design is treated in a stiff, lifeless manner and there is no trace of the naturalism which we find later on. One is at once struck by the marked resemblance which the design on this jar bears to the well-known dolphin fresco from Knossos. This fresco is reproduced in Plate XV owing to the kindness of Sir Arthur Evans, who has allowed me to make use of it, although he has not yet published it himself. From various evidence he assigns it to the M. M. III period to which our burial jar belongs. The similarities are striking, particularly in the treatment of the dolphins, which in both cases show the same horizontal wavy lines running along their sides and encircling the eyes.

It is clear that the maker of the Pachyammos jar was familiar with the great frescoes which covered the walls of the Minoan palaces in the M. M. III age, and that he attempted to reproduce them as nearly as possible on his clay pots. He made his mistake in not trying to modify and adapt the fresco painter's designs to suit the medium in which he was working, a thing which the L. M. I potters succeeded in learning shortly afterward.

The two remaining jars of this group were both drip pattern pithoi, one of which is shown in Pl. XVI, No. XII, c. The moulded "spectacle" pattern on the shoulder is unusual. It was near this group that the pithos was found which contained the intrusive child burial mentioned on page 15.

XIII. This group was composed of two M. M. I pithoi and

a pithos with drip pattern. One of the Middle Minoan pithoi was of the type shown in Pl. XI. The other jar is shown in Pl. XVII, No. XIII, a. The geometrical design in dark paint on a light ground is reminiscent of the light on dark ware of the preceding E. M. III period. (Vasiliki, Trans., Vol. II, Part 2, p. 120, Fig. 3, a and b, Fig. 5, c, and Fig. 6.) Other M. M. I examples of this style were found at Vasiliki. (Vasiliki, Trans., Vol. II, Part 2, pp. 126–28, Figs. 9, 10 and 11.) The design is in dark paint on the buff ground of the clay.

The drip pattern pithos from near this group contained two clay cups, one unpainted, the other with a band of white spirals on a dark ground, Pl. II, No. XIII, b. As I have said before, cups of this type are characteristic of the end of the M. M. III period and lasted on into the L. M. I age.

XIV. There were six jars in this group. The best of these is the fine amphora shown in Pl. XVII, No. XIV, a, and Pl. XVIII. It dates from the transition between the M. M. III and L. M. I periods. The bold design of bladder-like objects, spirals and plant motives is painted in brownish paint picked out in white on a light ground. The clay is greenish in color and very coarse in quality. It is hard to say what the design is really meant for. It may be a water plant like the lotus, of which we see the blossoms on tall, waving stalks, while the bladder-like object is the flower bud which has not yet reached the open air. Curious bladder patterns are common on L. M. I jars like those found at Pseira (Pseira, p. 33, Fig. 14), Mochlos (A. J. A., 2d series, Vol. XIII, p. 298, Fig. 19) and Gournia. (Gournia, Plates IX, No. 28, a and K.) It may be that the designs on these jars are a conventionalized form of the decorative motive found on our burial amphora, but if such is the case they have lost all the vigor of the original.

The white details which decorate the dark designs on the amphora are exceedingly charming and recall the delicate embroidery which one finds on the dress of the Knossian ladies in the palace frescoes of this same period.

This amphora and the jars of Plates IV, IX, XIV and XXI are the finest objects from the entire cemetery.

Owing to the shape and the narrow neck, this amphora must have contained either the body of an infant or the bones of an adult from which the flesh had been previously removed.

The remaining jars of this group are less interesting. Two of them were unpainted pithoi of the type of those shown in Pl. II. A third was a small unpainted pithos in poor clay, much rotted. The handles of this jar are oddly placed like those on the pithos of Pl. XI, No. I, c. The fifth jar of this group is shown in Pl. XVII, No. XIV, b. It is covered with black paint bearing bands of white on the shoulder and base. On the rim are incised two groups of five chevrons. This jar appears to be of M. M. III date and stood amid the fragments of a M. M. I pithos of the type of those shown in Pl. XI which had been broken up to make room for it. The sixth and last jar from this group is the small drip pattern pithos shown in Pl. XVI, No. XIV, c.

XV. This group was a curious mixture of pithoi placed at different depths. Near the surface stood an unpainted pithos with a moulded rope pattern on the shoulder containing an unpainted L. M. I cup. The bottom of this jar was so near the surface that it had been broken away quite recently in building a field wall. Near this pithos but a little deeper stood a pithos with drip pattern and close to it, lying on its side, was a large unpainted pot containing a plain clay cup of L. M. I date. This cup and the one mentioned above are of the type commonly classed with the L. M. I wares, though they might equally well belong to the previous period. They occur in great numbers on most Minoan sites. (Gournia, Pl. II, No. 13.)

At a still lower depth than the jars just mentioned stood the pithos of Pl. XII, No. XV, a. It lay entirely below sea level and from the rim of the jar to the surface of the beach was a depth of 2.50 m. This jar, which is of M. M. III date, was once covered with black paint and probably had some sort of white design, but of this no traces remain. It was embedded in a hard mass of solidifying sand as were most of the jars found at this depth. Near this jar at much the same depth stood the round bodied drip pattern pithos shown in Pl. XVI, No. XV, b. It contained two more unpainted L. M. I cups similar to those found in the other jars of this group. This pithos was embedded in the fragments of several earlier jars which had been broken up to make room for it.

XVI. This jar, Pl. XIX, No. XVI, which also lay very deep, bears traces of a white design on a dark ground and must belong to the M. M. III period. It is peculiar inasmuch as the spout is a false one and is not pierced through the wall of the vase. Beside it was found a small tripod of coarse red clay such as commonly occur in Minoan houses. (Gournia, Pl. II, Nos. 64, 72.) A small M. M. I amphora with white bands on a dark ground also came from this part of the site. This amphora and the tripod were too small to have served as burial jars and were evidently left there as offerings to the dead.

XVII. This group was composed of three larnakes and a pithos. The latter is similar to those of M. M. I date shown in Pl. XI. The larnakes are shown in Pl. XII, Nos. XVII, b and c, and Pl. XX, No. XVII, a. Of the three, No. XVII, a, is the most interesting. Its style of decoration, which is identical with that found on the jars of Pl. XI, places it in the M. M. I period.   These small chests all seem to have been provided with tightly fitting covers.   (See also No. XVII, c.) Nothing was found inside this chest, as the bones, probably those of a child, had quite disappeared.   It stood upright in the sand, although the large larnax of Pl. XII, No. XVII, b, which lay close beside it, had been buried upside down.   This also had a cover and inside were found a few fragmentary remains of human bones. (L. 93 cm., W. 42 cm., H. 30 cm.)   As I have said before (page 18), this large oval type of larnax is not likely to be later in date than the M. M. I period.

The small chest of Pl. XII, No. XVII, c, bears a drip pattern in white instead of the black paint that is commonly used for this design.   The white paint is of that yellowish quality so characteristic of the E. M. III period and quite different from the white employed by the Middle Minoan potters.   Thus it is possible that the chest is really of E. M. III date, which would make it somewhat earlier than the others of this group.   It contained no objects with the exception of very fragmentary skeletal remains.   Like No. XVII, a, it had been placed in the ground in an upright position.   (H. 28 cm., L. 40 cm., W. across top 24 cm.)

Larnakes appear so rarely in early deposits that it is curious to find three of them together as in this group.   In the Early Minoan and Middle Minoan cemeteries of Mochlos and Pseira no larnakes were found and at Sphoungaras the only one which came to light was of the square type of Pl. XII, No. X, a. (Sphoungaras, p. 34.)

Near this group a fourth chest, type of Pl. XII, No. XVII, c, in coarse red clay came to light.   This example, the clay of which was badly rotted, showed no traces of a painted design.

The following jars belonged to no well defined groups.

XVIII. This jar, Pl. XVII, No. XVIII, is a badly preserved example of the transition between the M. M. III and L. M. I periods. The body is divided into broad zones of dark paint worked out in white, alternating with zones filled with ripple pattern in dark paint on a light ground. The dark zones on the shoulder and middle of the jar bear spiral designs in white and on the dark band around the base are the traces of a wreath of white leaves.

XIX. A small jar of probably M. M. I or III date, Pl. XX, No. XIX. It seems to belong to the same general class of Middle Minoan jars as that shown in Pl. VIII, No. VIII.

XX. This jar, Pl. XX, No. XX, is evidently a somewhat later example of the type of jar shown in Pl. I, No. I, a. In shape it is more akin to the M. M. III and L. M. I jars of Pl. XIII, No. XI, b, and No. XII, a, and Plates VI, IX and X. On the other hand, the design is evidently derived from the motive which so frequently occurs on jars of the M. M. I period. (See Plates VII and XI.) On the whole, it seems reasonable to assign it to some time early in the M. M. III period.

XXI. This jar is shown in Pl. XX, No. XXI, a, and belongs to much the same date as the one just described. In fact, the remarks which apply to No. XX apply equally well to No. XXI, a.

Near this jar lay a pithos of the type of that shown in Pl. II, No. II, a, containing two clay cups, one of which was unpainted. (Gournia, Pl. II, No. 17.) The other cup is the one shown in Pl. XX, No. XXI, b. The design of spirals and bands is in white paint on a black ground. The surface is much worn. This cup belongs to the M. M. III or L. M. I period.

XXII. This jar which is shown in Plate XXI is one of the most beautiful from the entire cemetery. The simple yet very decorative wreath-like patterns in white on the black body paint of the vase date it without question to the M. M. III period. The treatment of the design is more finished and perhaps more conventional than is the case with the other painted jars from this cemetery. Nevertheless it has a quality which makes one feel that in the M. M. III period the Minoan civilization had reached or was about to reach the acme of its development.

There are, of course, many more jars from the Pachyammos cemetery but for the most part they are either unpainted or covered with the ordinary drip pattern. I regret to say that I have been obliged to publish this report without including illustrations of all the small cups and vases found with the jars and also without giving the exact dimensions of the jars themselves. The failure to include these is owing to the disturbed state of affairs now existing in Greece which has prevented my returning to Crete for the present. As the smaller vases are quite without interest or artistic merit, it has really mattered very little whether they were illustrated. In so far as it is possible I have given references to similar types of cups and vases which have been found on other sites.

In height the jars range from 40 to 90 centimeters. One jar was found which was a meter high, but this was unusual. The greater number of the painted jars are from 40 to 60 centimeters in height. The meter rule which appears in Plates V, VII, XVI and XIX shows the relative size of the jars in these groups.

I have to thank both Sir Arthur Evans and Dr. Duncan Mackenzie for their helpful suggestions, and also Mrs. Dohan (Miss Edith Hall), who has been kind enough to undertake the work of proof-reading.

PLATES

I-d

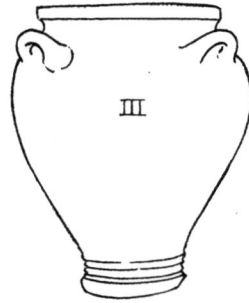

III

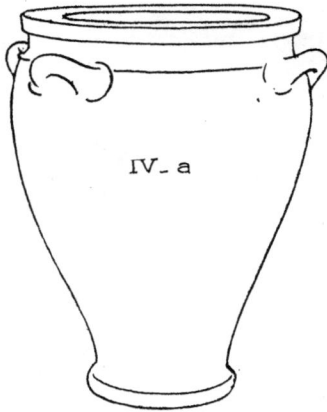

IV-a

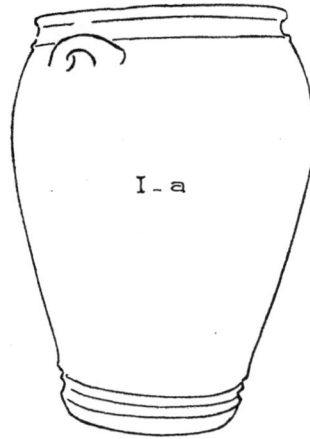

I-a

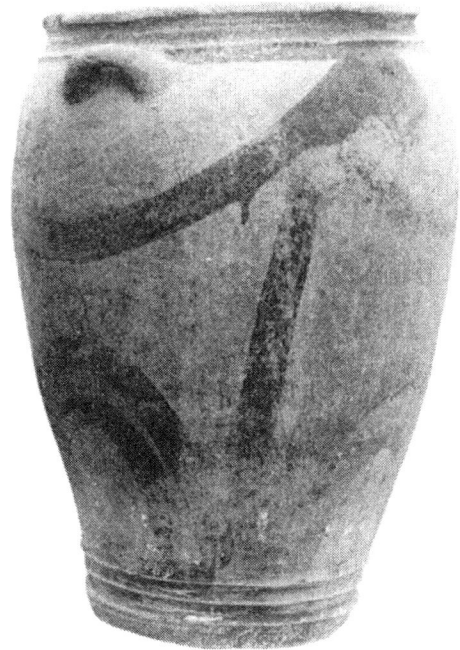

JARS OF VARIOUS PERIODS

XIII-b

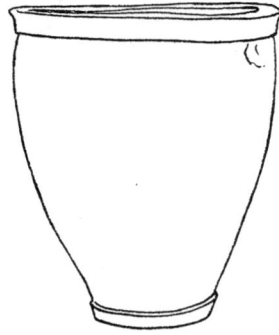

VI-a

I-b

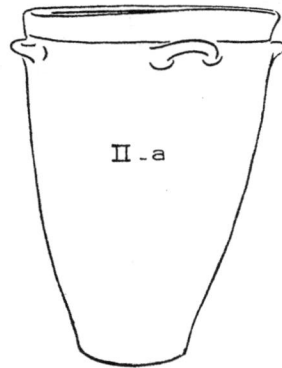

II-a

VESSELS OF VARIOUS PERIODS

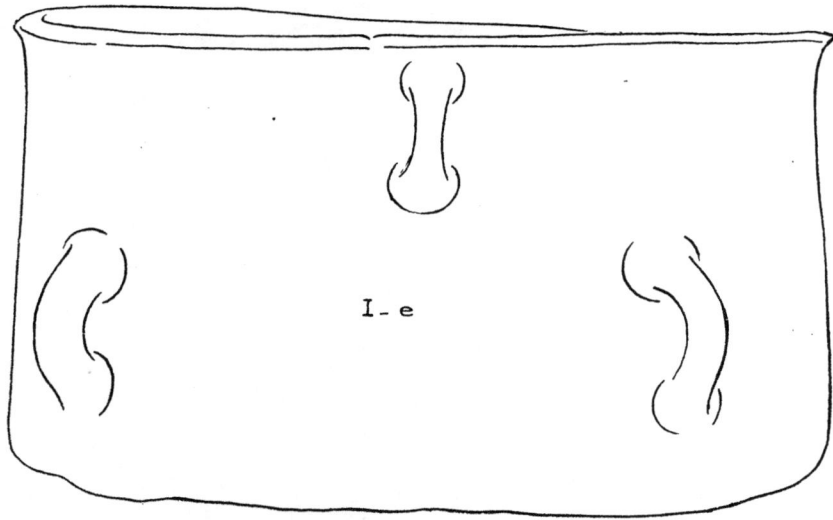

I_e

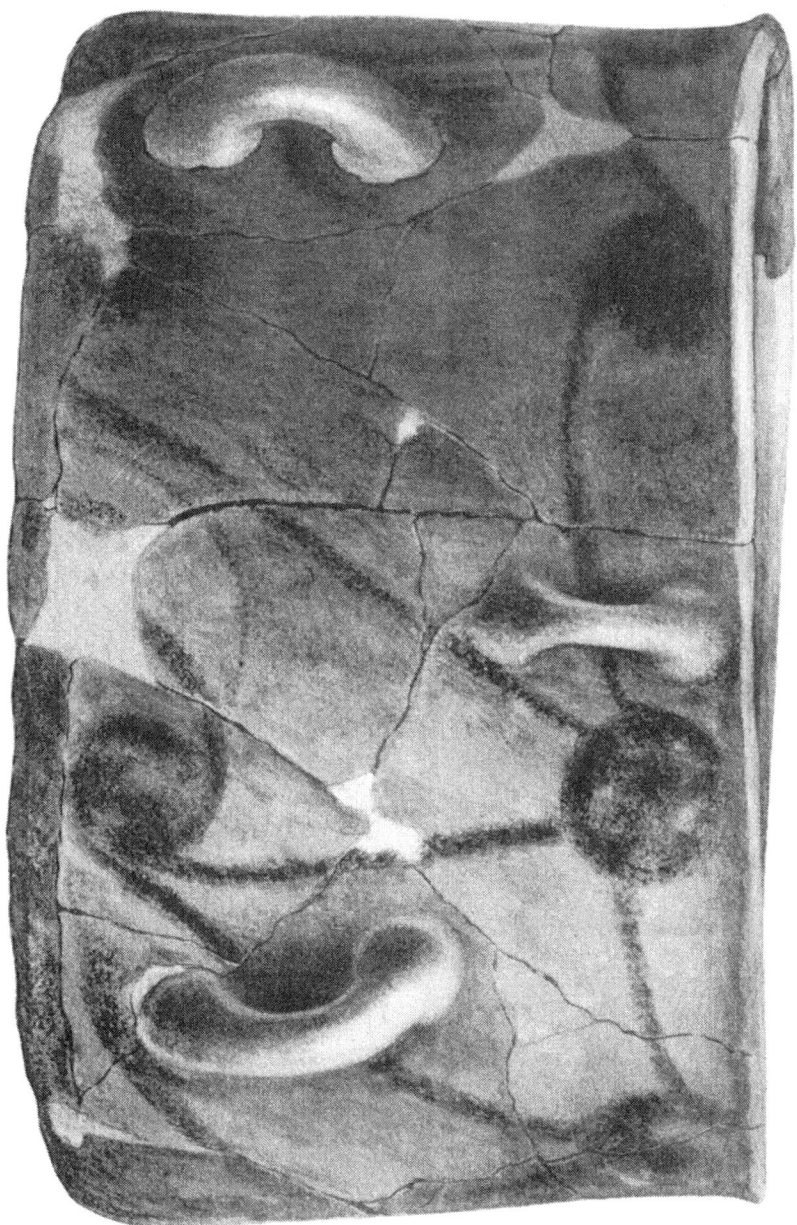

PLATE III

LARNAX, M. M. I PERIOD

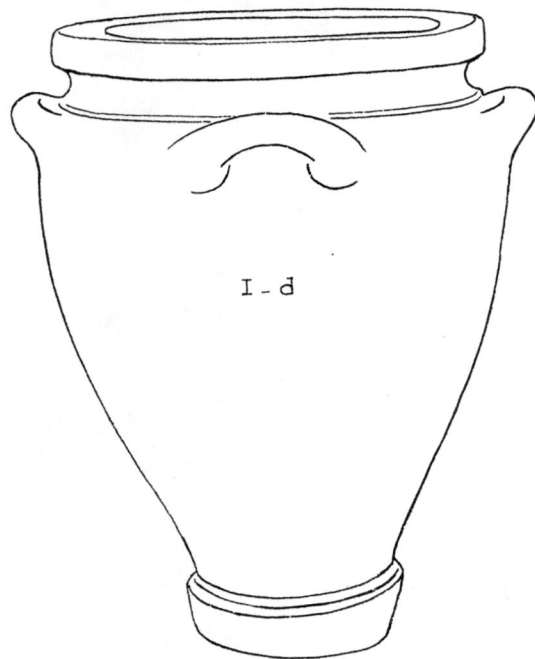

I - d

JAR, M. M. III PERIOD

PLATE V

GROUP OF JARS. M. M. III PERIOD

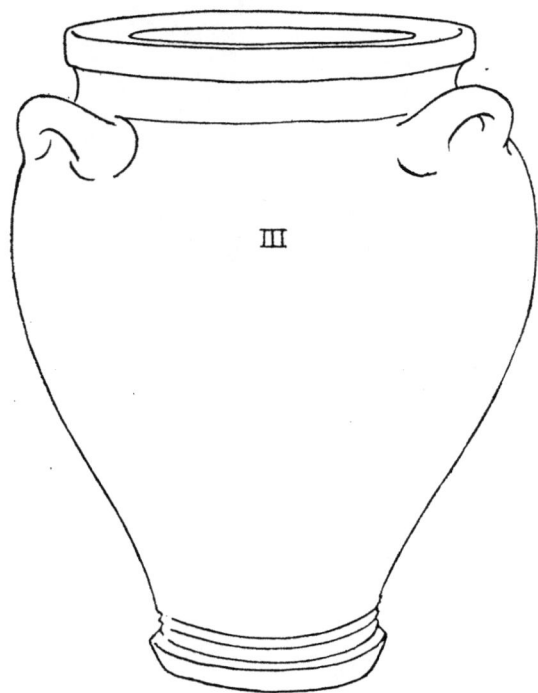

III

JARS OF TRANSITIONAL STYLE, M. M. III—L. M. I PERIODS

PLATE VII

JARS OF VARIOUS PERIODS

VIII

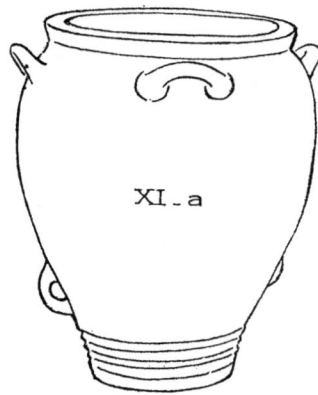

XI.a

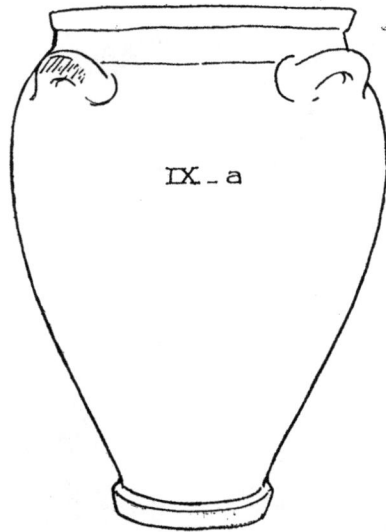

IX.a

JARS OF TRANSITIONAL STYLE, M. M. III—L. M. I PERIODS

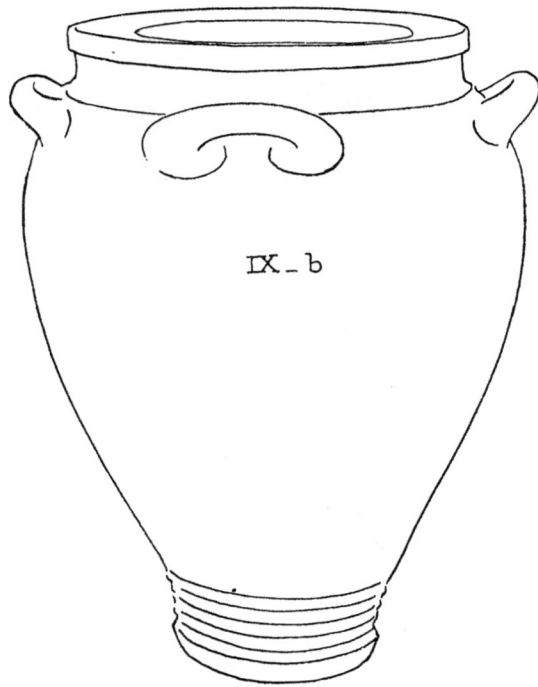

IX_b

VASE OF TRANSITIONAL STYLE
M. M. III – L. M. I PERIODS

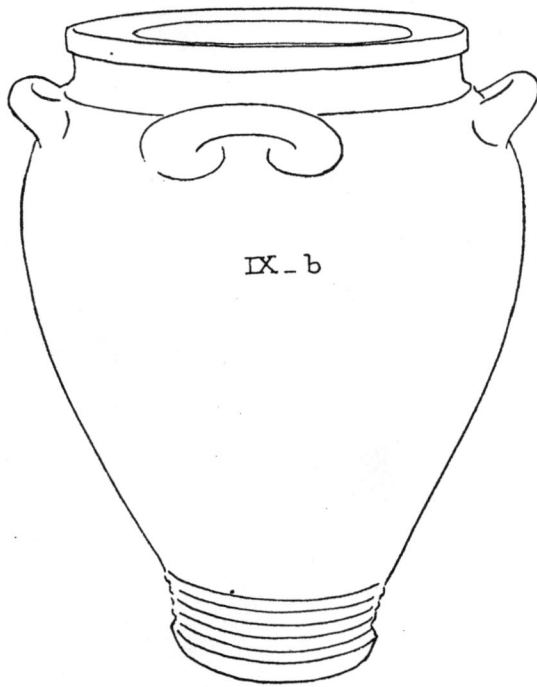

IX_b

PLATE X

JARS OF TRANSITIONAL STYLE, M. M. III—L. M. I PERIODS

XI_c

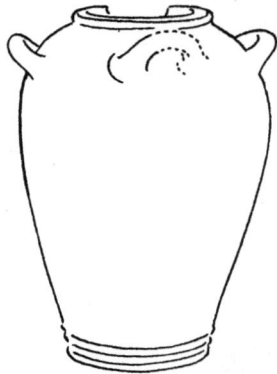

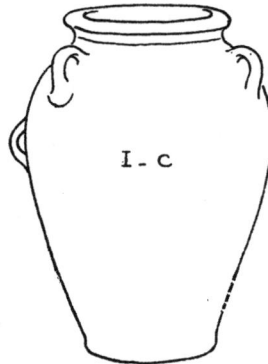

I_c

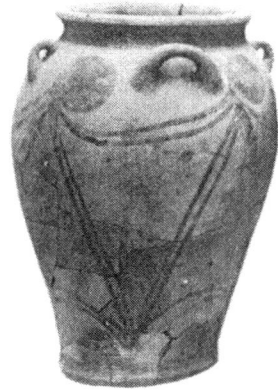

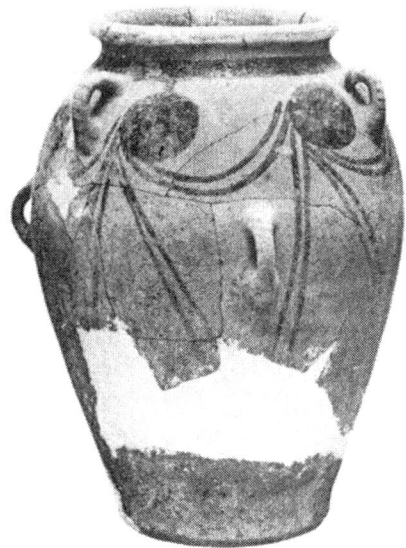

JARS OF E. M. III PERIOD AND M, M. I PERIOD

PLATE XII

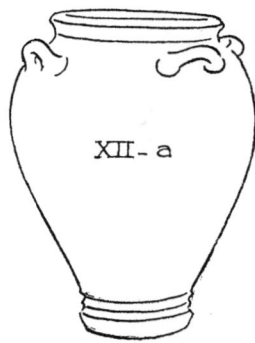

XII - a

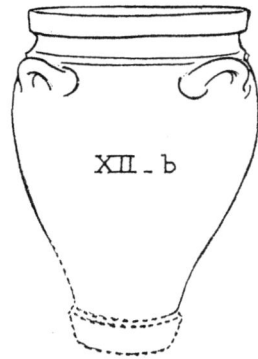

XII - b

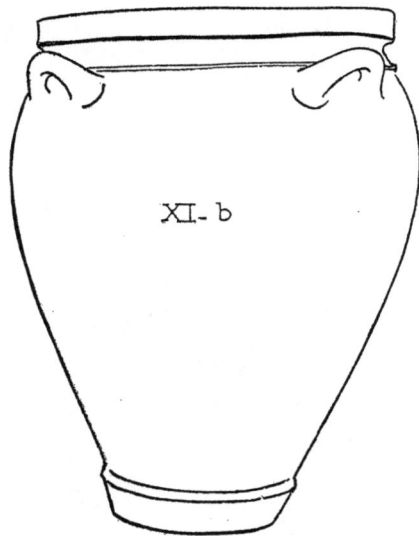

XI - b

JARS OF MIDDLE MINOAN PERIOD

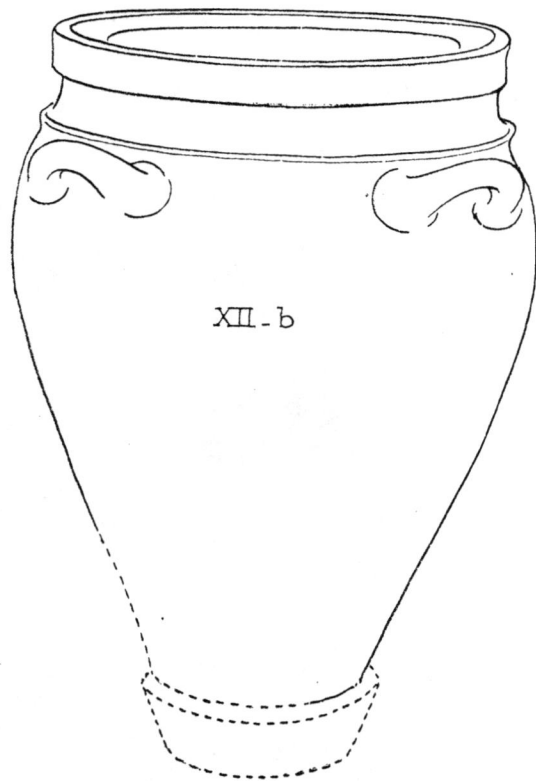

XII-b

JAR, M. M. III PERIOD

PLATE XV

ANTHR. PUB. UNIV. MUSEUM VOL. VII

FRESCO FROM KNOSSOS, M. M. III PERIOD.

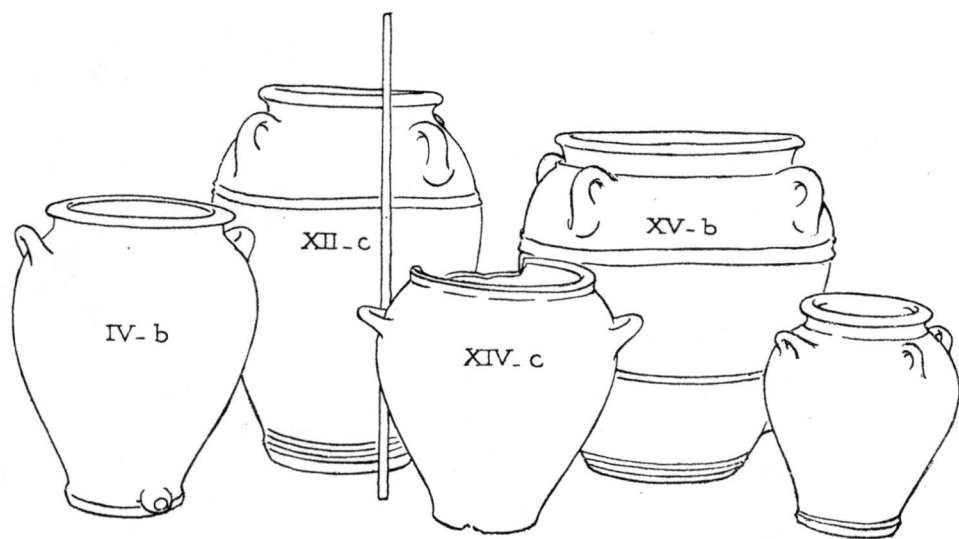

PLATE XVI

JARS OF VARIOUS PERIODS

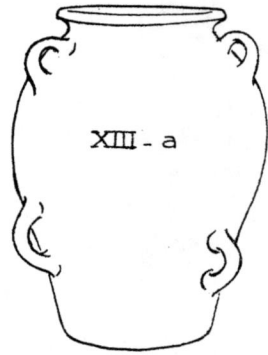

XIII - a

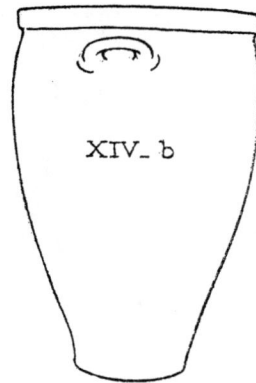

XIV - b

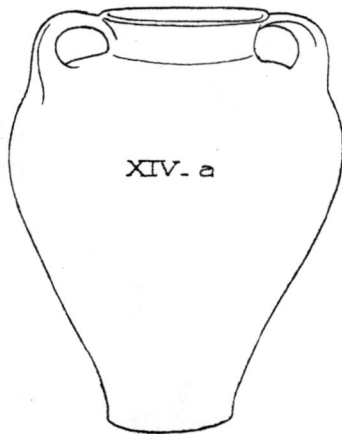

XIV - a

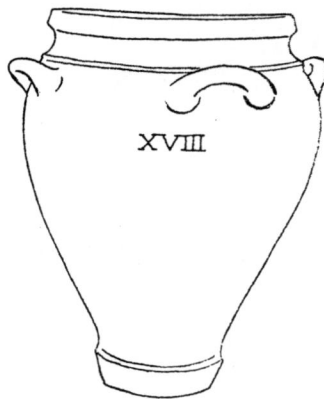

XVIII

JARS OF TRANSITIONAL STYLE, M. M. III—L. M. I PERIODS

VASE OF TRANSITIONAL STYLE
M. M. III – L. M. I PERIODS

PLATE XIX

JARS OF VARIOUS PERIODS

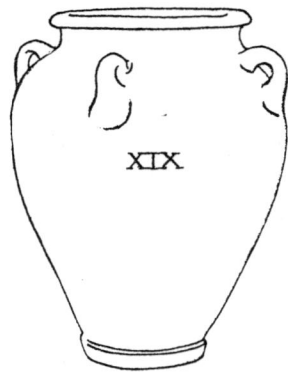

XIX

XXI_a

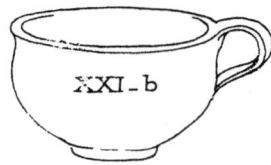

XXI_b

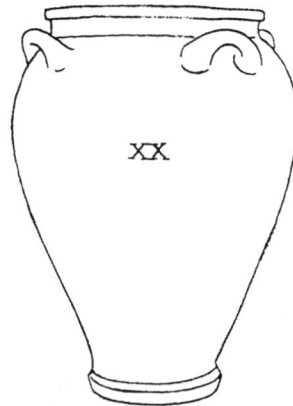

XX

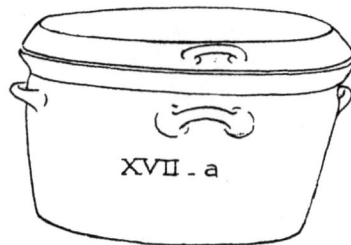

XVII_a

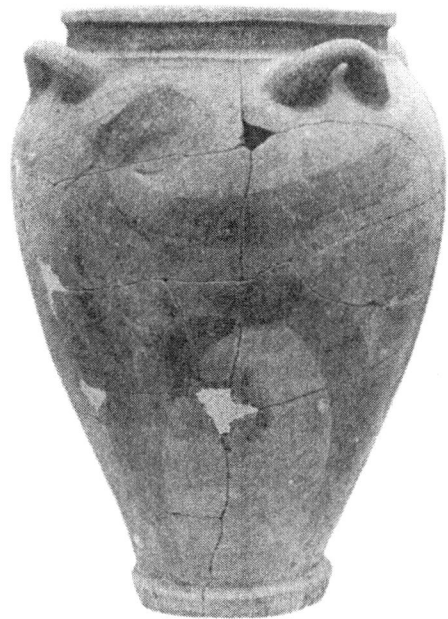

VESSELS, M. M. III PERIOD

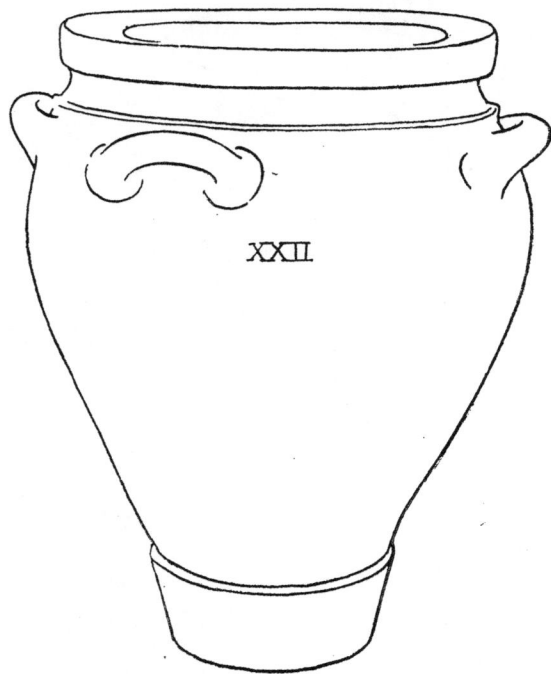

XXII

JAR, M. M. III PERIOD

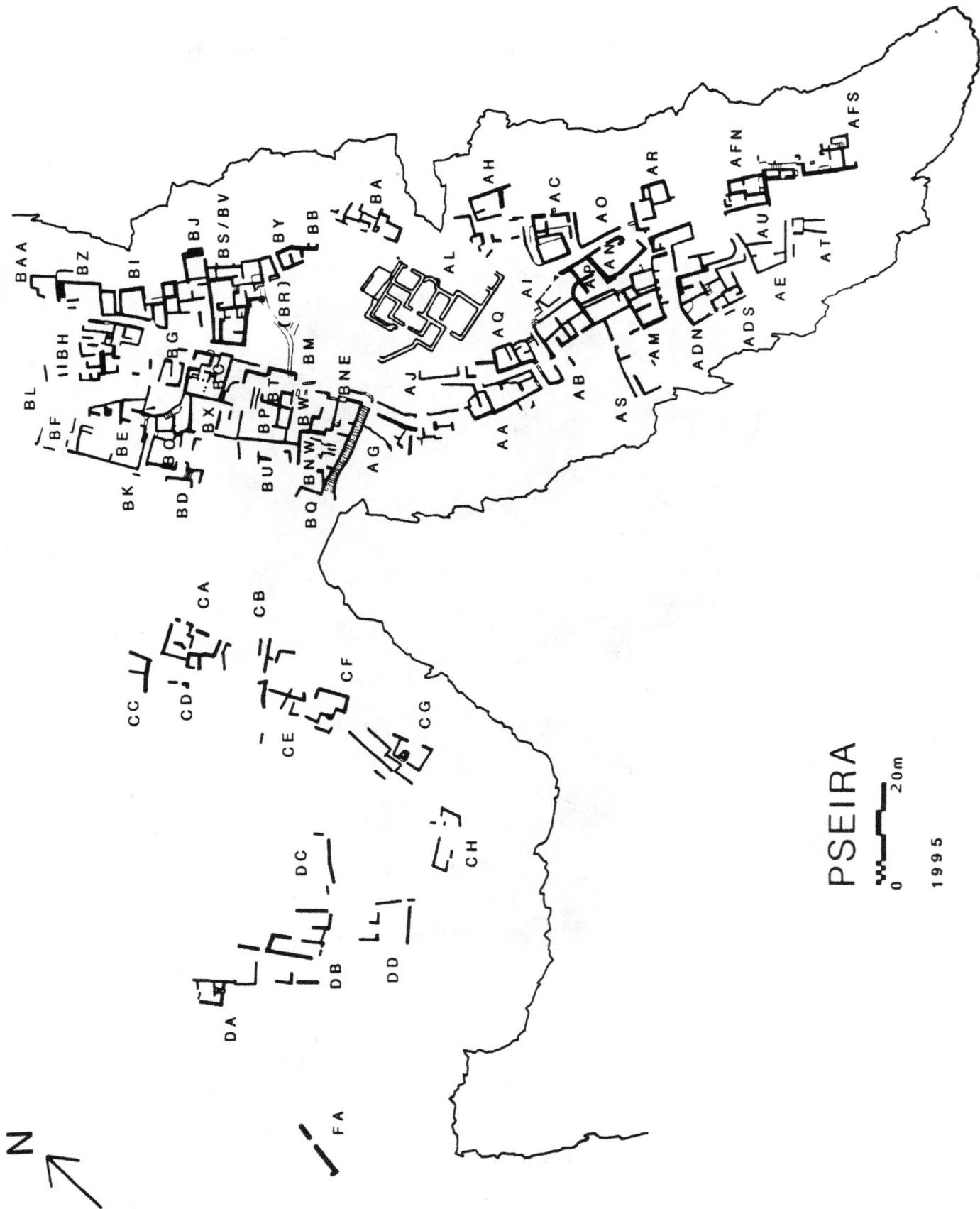

PSEIRA

0 20m

1995

N

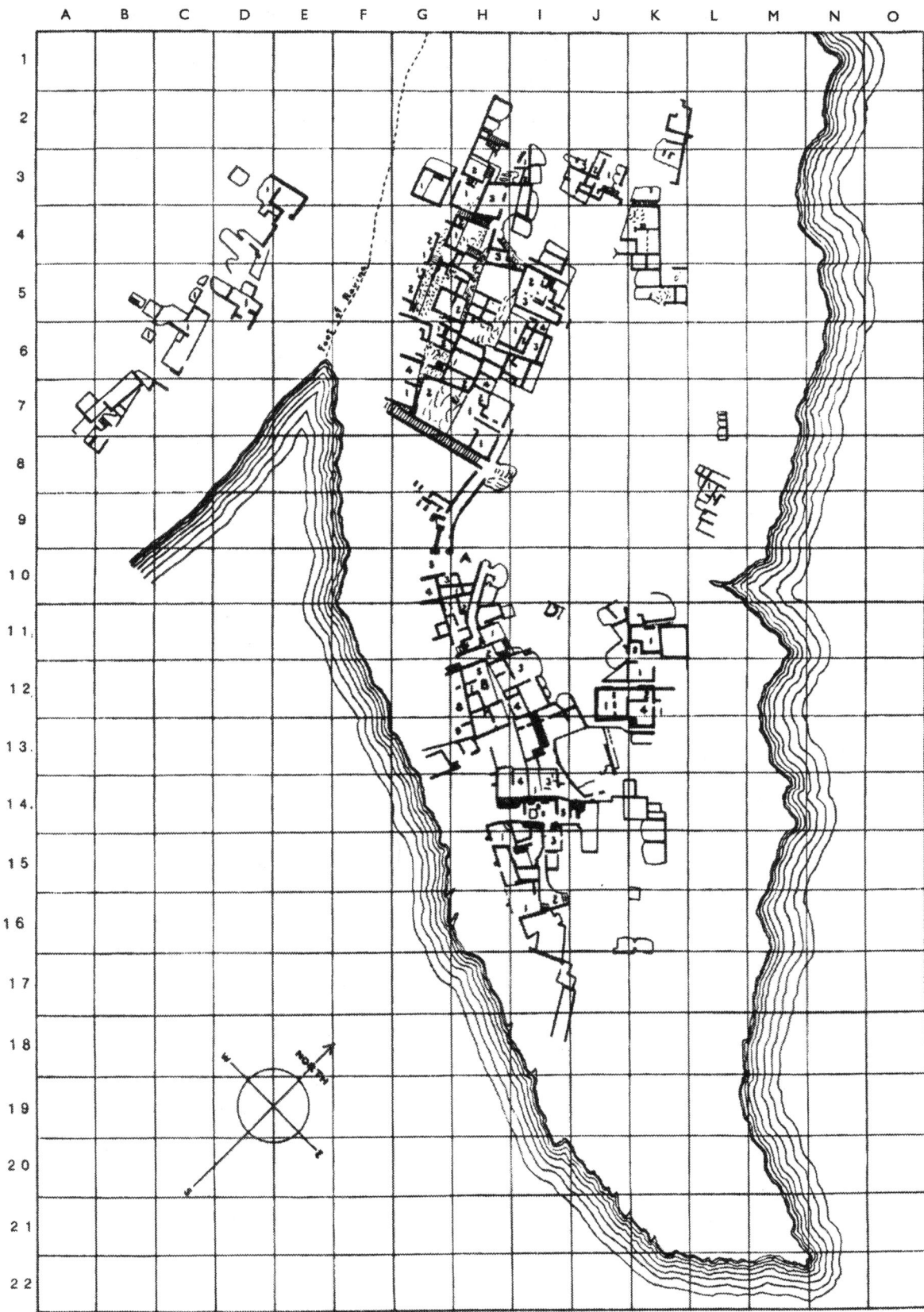

www.ingramcontent.com/pod-product-compliance
Lightning Source LLC
Chambersburg PA
CBHW080240270326
41926CB00020B/4311